SHARK ATTACK

SHARK ATTACK

Mac McDiarmid

SMITHMARK

Above: The well known diver and shark expert Valerie Taylor confronts a grey nurse shark.

This edition published in 1996 by SMITHMARK Publishers, a division of U.S. Media Holdings, Inc., 16 East 32nd Street, New York, NY 10016.

SMITHMARK books are available for bulk purchase for sales promotion and premium use. For details write or call the manager of special sales, SMITHMARK Publishers, 16 East 32nd Street, New York, NY 10016; (212) 532-6600

First published in Great Britain in 1996 by Parragon Books Limited
Units 13-17
Avonbridge Industrial Estate
Atlantic Road
Avonmouth
Bristol BS11 9QD
United Kingdom

Designed and produced by
Touchstone
Old Chapel Studio
Plain Road, Marden
Tonbridge, Kent TN12 9LS
United Kingdom

ISBN 0-7651-9698-0

Printed in Italy

Contents

Introduction
Page 6

Evolution of the Shark
Page 8

Types of Sharks
Page 10

Man-Eaters
Page 18

White Death
Page 22

Anatomy of a Killer
Page 30

Shark Senses
Page 34

Attack Methods
Page 38

**Shark Attacks –
a Global Overview**
Page 40

History of Attacks
Page 45

Attacks: Australia
Page 47

Attacks: North America
Page 50

Attacks: Pacific
Page 54

Attacks: New Zealand
Page 57

Attacks: Africa
Page 58

Attacks: Europe
Page 61

Attacks: Great Britain
Page 63

Attacks: Rest of the World
Page 64

Mass Attacks
Page 66

Provoked Attacks
Page 68

Victims
Page 71

Counter Measures
Page 76

Living with Sharks
Page 82

Shark Mythology
Page 86

'Jaws'
Page 88

Conclusion
Page 90

Index
Page 96

Introduction

'*THE SHARK hath not this name for nothing, for he will make a morsel of anything he can catch, master and devour.*'

Those words were written in 1655, by which time the shark was already a creature of myth and menace. Shark attack is probably as old as man's urge to go down to the sea, and the legends surrounding it can be little younger.

The first accurately documented attack occurred in 1580, when a seaman fell overboard on a voyage between Portugal and India. Despite stormy conditions, his shipmates managed to get a line to him, and he was almost back in the safety of the ship when, according to a contemporary account: '*a large monster called tiburon rushed upon the man and tore him to pieces before our very eyes. That surely was a grievous death.*'

There may be more grievous things in the ocean, but none carry quite the same sinister menace as the sub-order *Squali* of the order *Plagiostomi*: sharks. The sea itself is a killer: one minute benign, the next ferocious. It certainly claims innumerably more lives annually than all the man-eaters in history. Even amongst marine killers, the sea snake and the humble jellyfish exact a far higher toll on human life.

Perhaps part of the root of our horror is a grown-up version of a child's dread of the dark: fear of the unknown. For the killer shark can, and often does, strike without warning. Circling triangular fins are the exception, rather than the rule.

The shark, too, is an object of fascination, it's awful mastery of its element a reminder to us all that though man controls much of the planet, the sea is another domain. Few people can be unimpressed by the streamlined grace of a shark on the prowl, even if the thought does send a shiver of foreboding down our spines.

Comprehensive documentation of shark attack – and the urge to do something about it – began in earnest during World War II. Big, vicious fish were not only a hazard to shipwrecked sailors *per se*, they were bad for morale.

This came to a head after the sinking of the cruiser *Indianapolis* – ironically the very ship that delivered a horror of an even more terrible kind, the atom bomb – many of the survivors of which succumbed to shark attack. In 1942 the US Office of Strategic Services had initiated research into shark attack, with a view to identifying counter-measures. The result, 'Shark Chaser', was a repellent compound subsequently issued to service men for decades. Later evidence suggested sharks were indifferent to it, and even ate it, but for a time it bolstered morale.

In London, meanwhile, Winston Churchill, in answer to a parliamentary question about naval losses, declared his government 'entirely opposed to sharks'. He may as well have assured Fighter Command's potential casualties that he was equally opposed to gravity. The pronouncement was no doubt ironic, but must have come as slight relief to British mariners. A shark versus a bulldog, at sea at least, is no contest.

One of the problems, then and now, is that we understand so little of the beast in question. Even the origins of the word 'shark' are uncertain. In everyday life it is used to describe an assortment of con-men and charlatans, spivs and gigolos, although none

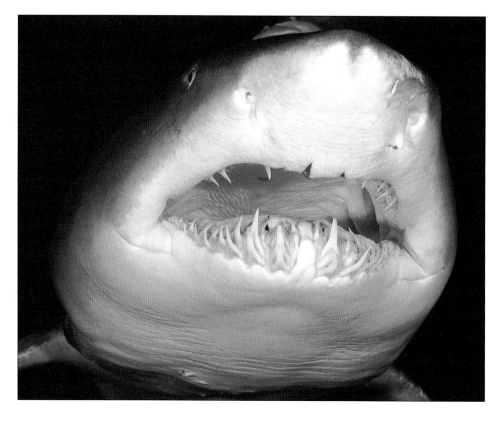

induces even a fraction of the horror aroused by the prototype. If anything, such usage is an insult to the sea-going variety which, if nothing else, is fearfully good at what it does.

Which brings us to the 'evil' behind those cruel fishy eyes. 'Good' and 'bad' are human judgements. A fish – any fish – simply does what it was designed to do by millions of years of evolution. Since one of the two fundamentals of any creature's existence is eating (the other being mating), perhaps we should be less quick to condemn when we carelessly dip a tasty morsel in his domain. I'm not suggesting we should welcome it, either, but the only 'good' or 'bad' that matters to a shark, is being good at being a shark. But sometimes, as Peter Benchley's *Jaws* so vividly suggested, the private life of the shark is also your biggest nightmare.

MEASUREMENTS

Many of the measurements of weights and lengths of sharks described in this book are estimates based on the reports of shark attack victims or eye-witness accounts. By their very nature, these figures are often rounded up to the nearest convenient figure and are represented in both metric and imperial equivalents.

Where more accurate measurements are available, they are duly recorded.

Below left: This normally benign grey nurse shark shows a fine array of teeth.
Above: An early engraving representing a hammerhead shark.
Below: A naturally graceful silky shark.

Evolution of the Shark

THE SHARK, whatever else it might be, is almost uniquely successful. According to fossil evidence, the earliest shark-like creatures prowled the world's oceans 450 million years ago – long before the age of dinosaurs. Compared to this, man's span of a couple of million years is a mere flash of a tiger shark's tail.

Evolution is the grindingly slow process which rewards success by 'survival of the fittest'. Organisms best suited to exploit their environment survive to breed, producing more like themselves. Those less suited to their surroundings fail to prosper and simply die out. If an environment changes, which may mean changes in predators or food supply, as well as physical surroundings, a species may need to adapt if it is to survive.

What happens in practice is that one or more of the myriad tiny differences that occur naturally in a population becomes an advantage or disadvantage. If the characteristic is an asset, the creature possessing it is more likely to survive and pass it on to the next generation. If it is not, the individual, and the characteristic, are more likely to die out. Humans, for instance, although all part of the same species, come in many shapes and sizes. Although modern man's capacity to change his environment has reduced his need to adapt to it, some of these could become more or less advantageous if our surroundings were to change.

Although the shark's environment, the sea, has probably been more constant than the one-third of the globe that is land, sharks, too, have undergone innumerable changes over the millennia. As Nature experimented to find her perfect fish, there were many successes but probably many more deadends. Some of these are preserved in layers of ancient rock, the 'fossil record', from where palaeontologists later unearth them.

Modern sharks almost certainly evolved from a group called *placoderms*, which experimented with a staggering variety of different jaw and fin forms.

Left: The fossilized jaws of the prehistoric shark Carcharodon megalodon.
Above: A set of enormous shark jaws and teeth from the Marquesas Islands.

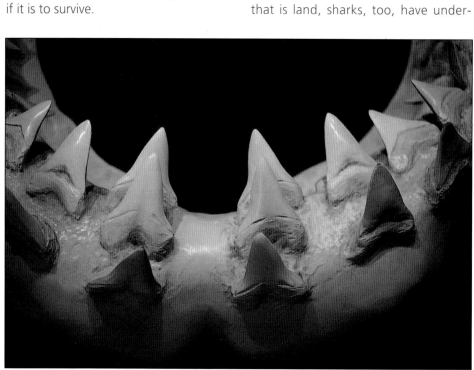

One of the first of these, *Cladoselache*, swam in a shallow ocean in what is now Kentucky, Ohio and Tennessee. About 1 metre (3ft 4in) long, it nonetheless had the familiar triangular fins, and a rakish tail not unlike the modern mako shark. But unlike the sharks of today, *Cladoselache* was but a bit-player in the ocean hierarchy, then ruled by the armoured *arthodires*, a huge carnivore up to 7 metres (23ft) in length. Palaeontologists speculate that speed and agility – two characteristics of its modern cousins – helped keep *Cladoselache* out of harm.

The early years of shark evolution produced a bizarre variety of creatures, some sporting elaborate dorsal fins, some great spirals of jagged teeth. Then, from about 300 to 150 million years ago, shark evolution appeared to slow down. Fossil sharks from this period fall into two main groups. *Xenacanths* were predominantly freshwater creatures, for a time hugely successful and distributed world-wide. However, around 220 million years ago, they became extinct.

The other group, the *hydobonts*, first appeared some 320 million years ago. Found in both salt and fresh water, these became extinct at about the same time as the dinosaurs. Indeed, *hydobont* and dinosaur fossils are occasionally found together in such places as Wyoming.

The earliest geological record of 'modern' sharks dates from about 100 million years ago. The creatures concerned had teeth not unlike today's mako and mackerel sharks. White shark-like teeth appeared some 65 million years ago.

The modern white shark is, of course, the most feared of them all. Originally, there appear to have been two sub-groups. One, with coarsely serrated teeth, probably evolved into the modern great white. The other had finely serrated teeth and included species of truly gargantuan size. The biggest, *Carcharodon megalodon*, exceeded 12 metres (40ft) in length. Its abundant teeth were as big as a man's hand. A photograph taken in New York's Museum of Natural History shows six men, two seated and four standing, comfortably accommodated in its awesome maw. Fortunately for us, these underwater giants reached their peak around 15 million years ago, and have long been extinct.

Below: A prehistoric shark tooth.

Types of Sharks

THE WORD 'shark', for all the singular terror it can inflict, encompasses a huge and varied array of individual species. Most of these will be unknown to the casual reader. Most, too, are regarded as harmless.

All sharks belong to the class *Chondrichthyes*, which also includes the rays. Modern sharks are divided into eight major groups or *orders*, each related by certain external characteristics. Within each order are one or more smaller groups, known as families. In total there are over 350 different species of shark, divided into 30 families.

RELATED SPECIES

Sharks are closely related to several other species, including rays, elephant fish and rat fish. Together they form the class *Chondrichthyes*, all of which share several distinctive features. Most notably, they have skeletons composed of cartilage rather than bone, and are sometimes referred to as cartilaginous fishes. All have nostrils and mouths on the underside of the head. They have a specialised form of scales (dermal denticles), giving the characteristic rough skin. All have *ampullae of Lorenzini*, a system for detecting minute electro-magnetic impulses in their surroundings. It is believed that sharks use this extra sense to locate their prey.

Comprising no less than 470 species, the rays are even more numerous than sharks. A few of these are dangerous to man, although the largest, the spectacular manta ray or devilfish, is a filter feeder which glides through the tropical oceans on its huge 'wings'.

MAN-EATERS

Amongst this array of 350 different shapes of potential terror, relatively few are known or suspected man-eaters.

Two of the ocean's most dangerous sharks; a tiger shark apparently ignores the attentions of a diver (left) and a great white in placid mood (above).

Half of all shark species grow to a maximum length of 1 metre (3ft 4in), whilst only one eighth routinely exceed 2 metres (6¹/₂ft). The best-known shark in British waters is the dogfish, probably the most widely-distributed of all the world's shark species.

Most sharks which attack humans belong to the family *Carcharhinidae*, also known, morbidly enough, as requiem sharks. The blue, whitetip reef shark, grey reef shark and tiger shark all belong to this group.

The largest and reputedly most ferocious of all sharks, the great white, belongs to a closely-related group, the mackerel sharks, to which the mako also belongs. The same order includes the thresher shark family.

DISTRIBUTION

Although sharks are distributed throughout the world's oceans (and one, the bull shark, is commonly found in the larger tropical rivers), they are chiefly creatures of warm water. Scientists divide shark species into three distribution groups: tropical, temperate and cold water sharks.

The tropical sharks are of the main interest to us. This group prefers waters warmer than 21°C (70°F) and includes most of the requiem sharks and the hammerheads. Many of these travel large distances daily, whilst some also migrate with the seasons – moving south during the northern winter, and vice versa.

Temperate water sharks inhabit waters with temperatures between 10° and 21°C (50°-70°F) and, like tropical sharks, their more active members often migrate. They include some requiem sharks, and the infamous great white, whose range includes the Bay of Biscay and the waters off Cornwall.

Cold water sharks live in waters colder than 10°C (50°F), which includes both the fringes of Arctic and Antarctic waters, and the chilly depths of warmer seas. These include the greenland shark, a large (up to 7 metres [23ft] in length) but sluggish creature widespread throughout British waters.

By far the most common sharks in the seas around British are various species of dogfish – once known, when served with chips on newspaper, as rock salmon. Perhaps the most celebrated is the basking shark (*Cetorhinus maximus*) which, like its tropical cousin the whale shark, feeds on small fish and plankton and is harmless to humans. This is just as well as examples of over 11 metres (36ft) in length have been recorded. At certain times of year these gentle giants are easily sighted in parts of the Irish Sea and off the Scottish coast.

NAMES

Latin names may be tiresome and hard to remember, but they are necessary. Sharks of the same species often enjoy a variety of local names. And those most dangerous to man, not surprisingly, are often saddled with the greatest variety of all. Sometimes these names overlap or flatly contradict each other. The great white (*Carcharodon carcharias*), for instance, is also called great blue, white pointer, plain white or, more sensationally, white death. Meanwhile the shortfin mako also answers to blue pointer, not to be confused with the blue shark.

1. Order *Squatiniformes*: ANGELSHARKS

Flattened, ray-like sharks, often found half buried in the sea-floor. About 13 species in all, ranging up to 2.4 metres (8ft) in length. Found in most cool temperate to tropical waters, including British seas. Bear live young.

2. Order *Pristiophoriformes*: SAWSHARKS

A single family of five species of harmless bottom-dwellers with distinctive saw-like snouts and a maximum length of around 1.5 metres (5ft). Bear live young.

3. Order *Squaliformes*: DOGFISH

Containing three families and over 80 species, these are marked by paired dorsal fins, no anal fin, and long snouts with short mouths. All bear live young.

3a. Family *Squalidae*: DOGFISH

Over 70 species, with huge varieties in size and shape, ranging from 30cm (1ft) to 6 metres (20ft) or more for the pacific sleeper and greenland sharks. Dogfish are mostly bottom-dwellers and widely distributed.

3b. Family *Oxynotidae*: ROUGHSHARKS

Five species of strange, stubby, almost pig-like sharks, generally under 1 metre (3ft 4in) long .

3c. Family *Echinorhinidae*: BRAMBLE SHARKS

Two species, the bramble shark and prickly shark, which grow to around 3 or 4 metres (10-13ft) respectively. Deep water dwellers.

4. Order *Hexanchiformes*: SIXGILL, SEVENGILL AND FRILLED SHARKS

A small group containing sharks with six or seven pairs of gill openings, an anal fin and a single spineless dorsal fin. Found mostly in deep water and bear live young which hatch from eggs within the body (ovoviviparous).

4a. Family *Chlamydoselachidae*: FRILLED SHARKS

Usually bottom-dwellers with slender eel-like bodies reaching a maximum length of around 2 metres (6½ft).

4b. Family *Hexanchidae*: SIX & SEVENGILL SHARKS

Four species with much heavier bodies and more shark-like appearance than the frilled sharks, their maximum lengths ranging between 1.5 and 5 metres (5-16½ft). Found mostly in deeper water in cold temperate to tropical seas. Take large prey, and some are also carrion feeders.

5. Order *Carcharhiniformes*: GROUNDSHARKS

By far the largest group with almost 200 species in eight groups. Although groundsharks, along with the mackerel sharks, provide most of the known man-eaters, they include many small and relatively docile species. Groundsharks have a long mouth and snout, two spineless dorsal fins and, most distinctively, movable lower eyelids.

5a. Family *Carcharhinidae*: REQUIEM SHARKS

A huge group of 48 sharks, moderately heavy-bodied and streamlined, with a pronounced upper caudal fin. Smaller species are under 1 metre (3ft 4in), although 3 metres (10ft) is common and the largest, the tiger shark, reaches 5 metres (16½ft) or more. Very widely distributed predator with a large range of habitats throughout the tropical and temperate seas, and usually the most numerous species in any particular location. All viviparous (bear live young), except the ovoviviparous tiger.

5b. Family *Sphyrnidae*: HAMMERHEAD SHARKS

Nine species with unique hammer-shaped heads. Most are small but the four largest reach up to 5 metres (16½ft). Viviparous.

5c. Family *Triakidae*: HOUNDSHARKS

Over 30 species, including the strikingly marked leopard shark. Mostly under 2 metres (6½ft) long. Most are bottom dwellers in shallow coastal waters, in all tropical and temperate oceans.

5d. Family *Leptochariidae*: BARBELED HOUNDSHARKS

A smaller species, similar to the true houndsharks, under 1 metre (3ft 4in).

Right: Don't try this at home, kids! An experienced diver hitches a ride on a tiger shark. Largest of the requiem sharks, tigers are widely distributed throughout tropical and temperate seas.

5e. Family *Hemigaleidae*: WEASEL SHARKS

Similar to the requiem sharks, this family comprises six species of coastal sharks, mostly confined to the Indian Ocean. Most are small, but the snaggle-tooth grows to 2.5 metres (8ft).

5f. Family *Scyliorhinidae*: CATSHARKS

Another large group with over 90 species, elongated, but mostly less than 1 metre (3ft 4in) in length. Most are bottom dwellers, often attractively camouflaged. Found in all but the Antarctic oceans. Oviparous.

5g. Family *Proscylliidae*: FINBACK CATSHARKS

Similar to the true catsharks. The largest, the smoothhound, usually reaches 1 metre (3ft 4in).

5h. Family *Pseudotriakidae*: FALSE CATSHARKS

Bearing a distinctive elongated dorsal fin, the false catshark is a bottom dweller favouring deep water. It grows up to 3 metres (10ft) in length and is ovoviviparous.

BRITISH MONSTERS

The largest shark commonly found in British waters is the basking shark (*Cetorhinus maximus*). Like the whale shark, this is a filter feeder and harmless to humans. Examples of over 11 metres (36ft) in length have been recorded.

---

6. Order *Lamniformes*: MACKEREL SHARKS

Comprising around fifteen species in seven families, the mackerel sharks appear to be unique in combining a form of ovoviviparous reproduction with intrauterine cannibalism (see chapter **Anatomy of a Killer**). Most have long snouts and mouths, and are widely distributed throughout all but the polar oceans.

6a. Family *Lamnidae*: MACKEREL SHARKS

Five species of large, heavy-bodied sharks, the largest of which is the notorious great white but also including the shortfin mako. Sizes range from 3 to over 6 metres (10-20ft). Mackerel sharks are widely distributed in mainly coastal waters, in cool temperate to tropical seas, and bear live young.

Above: This nurse shark displays its armoury of razor-sharp teeth – designed for devouring fish, rather than attacking humans.

Above: An oceanic white tipped shark is silhouetted against a radiant sun.

6b. Family *Alopiidae*: THRESHER SHARKS

Three species of stout-bodied sharks, most easily recognised by a the huge upper lobe of their caudal fin. They range from 3 to 6 metres (10-20ft) in length. Chiefly found in deeper water, thresher sharks occupy all tropical and temperate seas.

6c. Family *Odontaspididae*: SAND TIGER OR RAGGED-TOOTH SHARKS

Three or four species of large, heavy-bodied sharks, all over 3 metres (10ft) in length. Although often found in deep water, all are coastal dwellers. Includes the so-called grey nurse, also known as the sand tiger.

6d. Family *Cetorhinidae*: BASKING SHARKS

Huge, heavy bodied filter-feeder with gill openings almost encircling the head. Many reach 10 metres (33ft) in length, with sightings of specimens estimated at 15 metres (50ft). Most common in cool temperate waters, including British, and even close inshore

6e. Family *Megachasmidae*: MEGAMOUTH SHARKS

Large (over 4 metres [13ft]), little-known, heavy bodied shark with a huge mouth and blunt snout. Thought to be confined to the Pacific Ocean.

6f. Family *Mitsukurinidae*: GOBLIN SHARKS

An ugly character with a spike-like snout above a long protruding upper jaw and an elongated caudal fin with no upper lobe. A bottom-dweller of around 3.5 metres (11½ft) in length, goblin sharks are rare but are scattered throughout most oceans.

6g. Family *Pseudocarchariidae*: CROCODILE SHARKS

So called because of its prominent teeth, the crocodile shark has a stream-lined body, exaggerated caudal fin and huge eyes. It grows to a little over 1 metre (3ft 4in) in length and its patchy distribution extends through most oceans.

7. Order *Orectolobiformes*: CARPETSHARKS

Carpetsharks are warm-water fish, comprising some 33 species in seven families, living mainly in the western Pacific and Indian oceans. All have catfish-like barbels adjacent to their nostrils.

7a. Family *Hemiscylliidae*: LONGTAILED CARPETSHARKS

At least 12 species with moderately broad bodies, greatly elongated tails and, sometimes, strikingly patterned bodies. Rarely over 1 metre (3ft 4in) long. Reef and bottom-dwellers, probably oviparous, and widely distributed throughout the Indian ocean and western Pacific.

7b. Family *Parascylliidae*: COLLARED CARPETSHARKS

Seven species of patterned sharks with long, slim bodies and tails, all under 1 metre (3ft 4in) in length. Confined to the western Pacific. Probably oviparous.

7c. Family *Orectolobidae*: WOBBEGONGS

Six species of broad, flattened, highly camouflaged bottom-dwellers, mostly found around New Guinea and Australia. Ovoviviparous. Some grow to over 3 metres (10ft), but most are smaller.

7d. Family *Ginglymostomatidae*: NURSE SHARKS

Three species, ranging in length from only 75cm (2½ft) to the 3 metre (10ft) tawny and nurse. Familiar bottom-dweller found in all tropical oceans, with broad heads and moderately sturdy bodies and tails. The nurse shark itself, at least, is ovoviviparous. The so-called grey nurse belongs to another family, the mackerel sharks.

7e. Family *Brachaeluridae*: BLIND SHARKS

Two species, broadly similar in appearance to collared carpetsharks, but slightly sturdier and with a more rearward anal fin. Reef dwellers in Australian waters, they grow to over 1 metre (3ft 4in) and are ovoviviparous.

7f. Family *Stegostomatidae*: ZEBRA SHARKS

A single species, with a striking broad caudal fin, sometimes exceeding 3 metres (10ft) in length. They lay eggs and inhabit reef areas throughout the western Pacific and Indian oceans, feeding mainly on small crustaceans.

7g. Family *Rhiniodontidae*: WHALE SHARKS

The largest of all sharks, this mottled, broad-headed monster is a filter-feeder eating plankton and small fish. It is found in all tropical and warm temperate seas and grows to 18 metres (60ft) in length. It is unclear whether it is oviparous or ovoviviparous.

8. Order *Heterodontiformes*: BULLHEAD SHARKS

The eight species of bullhead sharks uniquely combine paired, spined dorsal fins and an anal fin. They have large, broad heads with pronounced brow-crests, and range between around 50cm (1ft 8in) and 1.6 metres (5ft 3in) in length. Oviparous (egg-laying), they are mainly confined to the Indian and Pacific oceans.

Right and below: The massive whale shark is a gentle giant, using its broad mouth to filter-feed on plankton.

THE LARGEST FISH

The whale shark (*Rhincodon typus*), the largest fish, grows to over 18 metres (60ft) in length and over 40 tonnes/tons in weight. Like the largest whales, it is a plankton feeder. The biggest on record was taken in the Gulf of Siam in 1991. It was 18.5 metres (60ft 8in) long and weighed 43 tonnes/tons.

The whale shark also lays the largest egg of any living species. One measuring 25 x 14 x 9cm (10 x 5 x 3in) was discovered in the Gulf of Mexico. It contained an embryo almost 36cm (1ft 2in) long.

Man-eaters

OF THE 350 species of shark, the vast majority are harmless to human beings. But of the 30 or so species known to be dangerous, the main common characteristic – like that often cited of human offenders – is opportunity: their habitat overlaps that of man.

It is not simply a shark species' distribution north-to-south which contributes to its potential for man-eating, but its general habits and its macro-distribution. To be a man-eater, a shark – or any other carnivore – must come into contact with people, at least occasionally. It needs to inhabit regions where people habitually visit the water, whether out of necessity or recreation. It probably helps if it is an 'active' shark rather than a bottom dweller. And its threat inevitably increases with size: most dangerous sharks are over 1.8 metres (6ft) in length.

The great white, examined in more detail in the next chapter, fits all these bills. Although it avoids equatorial waters, the species is widespread from the southernmost tip of New Zealand to Alaska. Active it certainly is, yet it is also unusually confined to coastal waters and continental shelves – precisely those areas where people most commonly meet the sea. Perhaps the reputation of the great white rests as much on this unhappy accident as on the innate viciousness of the beast.

MAN-EATERS

All sharks eat and, however emotive an expression 'man-eater' might be to us, to a shark we are simply one more dietary constituent of the world's oceans. It is simply not known whether certain species of shark 'prefer' a human element to their diet, although judging by the assorted junk sometimes removed from sharks' stomachs, taste is not necessarily a factor.

Our good fortune, on a globe of which two-thirds is water and the shark is king, is that we live predominantly on land. Our bad luck is that when we do venture into the oceans it is we that become the proverbial fish out of water. If not strictly mouth-watering, a swimming human being must be a deliciously easy target to the sea's bigger carnivores. Put like that, perhaps the surprise is that more of us do not end up on a shark *à la carte*.

LITTLE & LARGE

Swallowing an adult human being whole takes a very large shark indeed and is probably a very rare occurrence. Of the 1652 cases examined in the US Navy Shark Attack file, only six such examples were confirmed.

But even tiny sharks can be aggressive. A shark researcher was once bitten sharply on the finger by an unborn sand tiger pup as he examined its pregnant mother.

Left: In Australia, this relatively small shark is known as the bronze whaler, and is considered to be responsible for attacks on bathers and surfers.

KNOWN MAN-EATERS: THE MAJOR CULPRITS

TIGER SHARK
Galeocerdo cuvier

Other than the great white, the tiger shark is considered the most aggressive to man, and certainly the most dangerous of all sharks in tropical waters. Seemingly indiscriminate in its choice of prey, this 'garbage can with fins' seems prepared to devour almost anything it encounters – even car parts have been found in tiger sharks' stomachs. It grows to over 5 metres (16½ft) in length yet is sometimes found in water less than 2 metres (6½ft) deep. Tiger sharks possess distinctive scimitar-shaped, curved, jagged teeth.

BULL SHARK
(Zambezi shark)
Carcharhinus leucas

The bull shark is unique amongst suspected man-eaters in that it often frequents tidal estuaries and even freshwater rivers in tropical and subtropical zones. This, and its preference for shallow coastal waters, inevitably puts it into close proximity to man. Fatal attacks in Lake Nicaragua have been attributed to the bull shark. Although the bull grows to no more than 3.5 metres (11½ft) and is less physically impressive than many man-eaters, it is now regarded as a particularly aggressive and dangerous species – second only to the tiger in warm seas. It's serrated triangular teeth are sometimes mistaken for great white's.

BLUE SHARK
Prionace glauca

The blue shark is a pelagic (deep water) species widely distributed throughout the world's warm temperate and tropical seas. Tagging has shown that individuals roam thousands of miles. Fast and aggressive, its oceanic nature makes it the most obvious culprit in attacks on shipwreck survivors where it can attack without provocation and often in some numbers, especially when aroused by blood in the water. Attacks in inshore waters, however, are highly unlikely. The blue shark grows to almost 4 metres (13ft) in length and is a relative of the tiger and bronze whaler sharks.

Above: The blue shark is distributed throughout the world's oceans and is a fast, efficient killer, thought to attack shipwreck survivors in open water.

COPPER SHARK
(Bronze Whaler)
Carcharhinus brachyurus

Another coastal shark widespread in warm temperate waters, the copper shark is known in Australia as the bronze whaler, whilst Americans call it the narrowtooth shark. Although comparatively small at 2.4 metres (8ft), it is believed to have been responsible for several attacks on bathers and surfers.

RISKY, FRISKY!

Fishermen are at particular risk because their work can put them in daily contact with injured sharks – and a shark can remain capable of inflicting injury even 30 minutes after it has been removed from the water.

SHORTFIN MAKO
Isurus oxyrinchus

A member of the same mackerel shark order as the great white, the shortfin mako has a similar heavy, spindle-shaped body although it is substantially shorter at some 4 metres (13ft). It is a prized game fish due to its acrobatic and spectacular responses when hooked. The same speed which gives this capability makes it a fearsome attacker, and it can be equally belligerent once landed. Several mako 'attacks' have occurred on board fishing boats. It is widespread throughout offshore temperate and tropical waters.

HAMMERHEAD SHARKS
Sphyrna spp.

Most of the nine species of hammer-heads are harmless to man, but the three largest are not. The great (*S. mokarran*), smooth (*S. zygaena*) and scalloped (*S. lewini*) hammerhead are all considered dangerous; the former grows to around 6 metres (20ft) in length, the latter 2 to around 4 metres (6½-13ft). Most descriptions, however, depict them as surprisingly timid creatures which rarely attack unless provoked. Hammerheads are distributed throughout the coastal margins of all warm temperate and tropical seas. They usually stay at some depth, venturing into shallow water to feed.

Below: A large hammerhead shark is silhouetted against the water's surface. Right: Divers toy with a tiger shark in the clear water of the Bahamas.

Analysis of the Shark Attack file gives a median length of 2.1 metres (6ft 10in) for attacks in which the length of the shark was reliably estimated. The shortest attacker was a mere .5 metre (1ft 8in) long, whilst six exceeded 6 metres (20ft).

KNOWN ATTACKERS OF HUMANS
(From US Navy Shark Attack File)

ORDER HEXANCHIFORMES
Sevengill shark	1

ORDER HETERODONTIFORMES
Horn shark	1

ORDER SQUALIFORMES
Family Orectolobidae – carpet sharks
Carpet sharks, unspecified	6
Nurse shark	15
Wobbegong	15

Family Odontaspididae – sand tigers
Sand sharks, unspecified	6
Ragged-tooth	5
Grey nurse, all types	20

Family Alopiidae – thresher sharks
Thresher shark, unspecified	1

Family Lamnidae – mackerel sharks
Great white sharks	32
Mako sharks, all types	18
Bonito shark	3
Salmon shark	1
Mackerel shark	2

Family Carcharhinidae – requiem sharks
Whaler sharks, unspecified	8
Tiger sharks, all types	27
Blacktip shark, unspecified	8
Blue sharks, all types	12
Bronze whaler	8
Bull sharks, all types	21
Other requiem sharks	31

Family Sphyrnidae – hammerhead sharks
Hammerheads, all types	13

In addition to the species described in the table, at least 18 other species of requiem shark have been cited in 31 attacks on humans.

ROGUE SHARKS

Several shark experts have advanced 'rogue shark' theories reminiscent of similar notions about man-eating tigers which develop a taste for human flesh. Study of shark attack patterns sometimes reveals 'bunches' of attacks in areas which have seen no such hazard for years, and which appear to cease as suddenly as they began.

One such episode took place off the Queensland coast of Australia in 1983. Three people were left in the water when their boat, the *New Venture*, sank. Gathering together various wreckage, including a surfboard, they assembled a makeshift raft and paddled towards help.

After several hours, what they believed to be a tiger shark, 5 metres (16½ft) in length, began to harass the trio. Eventually, it struck at the captain, Ray Boundy, who was able to deter it with a well-directed kick.

Some minutes later the shark returned, making a determined attack on Dennis Murphy, who reported that he had lost a leg. Murphy courageously urged his companions to make their escape, since he believed his wounds were fatal. They did so, but saw Murphy's body thrown out of the water and eaten by the tiger.

Two hours later the shark struck again, biting Linda Horton around the upper body, and shaking her before dragging her under. Boundy was shortly able to reach a nearby reef, from where he was later rescued by helicopter.

White Death

POSSIBLY no other shark – perhaps no other creature still living – arouses quite the same sense of horror as Mr 'Jaws' himself: the great white shark. Although there is no universal agreement on the common name of *Carcharodon carcharias*, on one thing every seafarer does concur: this two tonne/ton torpedo of muscle and teeth is every inch the ultimate predator.

Ever since it rose to Hollywood stardom in the movie *Jaws*, the great white shark has been the daddy of them all – the man-eater's man-eater. It is unquestionably the most dangerous shark species in temperate waters, with a northern hemisphere range extending from Senegal to Cornwall, and in North America from Mexico to Alaska.

Above all, the great white is big. Estimates as great as 11 metres (36ft) have been documented, but these are probably unreliable. Yet the reality is almost as terrifying. The largest example ever caught, harpooned off the Azores in 1978, was 9 metres (29½ft) in length and over 4.5 tonnes/tons in weight. For comparison, a typical adult African bull elephant weighs only 1 tonne/ton more.

The Azores great white measured 4.17 metres (13ft 8in) across its pectoral fins, whilst each of its wickedly serrated teeth was 7.6cm (3in) tall. Teeth as large as 15cm (6in) have been recovered from the ocean floor, suggesting that great whites much larger than the Azores specimen exist, or have in the relatively recent past. Yet even a medium-sized great white has stupendous biting power, estimated at three tonnes per square centimetre (which equates to approximately 26 tons per square inch).

ANATOMY

The great white is the biggest of all predatory sharks, one of a relatively small family of five species, the *Lamnidae* or mackerel sharks. The family name has nothing to do with diet, but arises instead from small mackerel-like stabilising keels on each side of the tail fin. As well as the great white, the family comprises the shortfin and longfin mako, the salmon and porbeagle sharks. The shortest grows to over 3 metres (10ft) in length, and all are potential man-eaters.

The *Lamnidae* are stouter in body form than the 'typical' shark, with a near-perfect hydrodynamic shape. Their metabolism is also more sophisticated than most shark species.

As well as larger hearts, accounting for around 0.2 per cent of total body-weight (compared to a more typical 0.1 per cent), the mackerel sharks maintain a body temperature significantly higher than their surroundings. Whilst not making them strictly warm-blooded, this temperature elevation – 5-11°C (8-20°F) above ambient – gives more efficient muscle operation, particularly in colder waters. A complex circulatory system helps to reduce heat loss.

Mackerel sharks also have a higher than usual proportion of red to white muscle, and sited deeper in body. Red muscle, like ours, has an abundant blood supply and is used when the shark is cruising rather than for rapid bouts of fast swimming. Mackerel sharks are thus designed for patrolling great distances.

The great white was once thought to feed principally on seals and sea lions – and that much of its danger to man arose because it mistook us for the same. However, more recent evidence suggests that it also eats tuna, turtles, dolphins and even takes chunks out of whales. The likelihood, far more chilling, is that *Carcharodon carcharias* will take whatever it can catch.

This illustrates how little we really know about this giant fish. Its breeding habits are almost unknown, and the few attempts to keep the creature in captivity have failed dismally. One example lay at the bottom of its tank and died 35 hours after it arrived; a second became so obviously distressed and disorientated that it was released after three days.

LARGEST MAN-EATER

The largest man-eater ever caught was a great white shark (*Carcharadon carcharias*) weighing over 4536kg (4½ tons). It was harpooned off the Azores in June 1978. The shark was no less than 9 metres (29½ft) in length. For comparison, a typical adult bull elephant weighs around 5500kg (5½ tons).

Right: Very big and very dangerous, a great white shark surfaces to show the full horror of those jaws that have earned this terrifying creature the title 'white death'.

Overleaf: A great white advances towards the stern of a shark investigation boat, whilst the diver seems blissfully unaware, inside the relative safety of a metal 'shark-proof' cage.

DISTRIBUTION

The distribution of great white attacks is considerable, as befits a particularly wide-ranging type of shark. Although it is not found in equatorial regions, the great white is common off both coasts of North and South America, Australia (except the north coast), New Zealand, Atlantic north Africa and Europe as far north as Cornwall, the Mediterranean, and the western Pacific from Taiwan to North Korea. Like all large predators, it is almost certainly not numerous.

Within these limits the great white appears to prefer coastal waters – another factor which increases the likelihood of encounters with man. It is generally thought to prefer water deeper than 30 metres (100ft), so is more likely to be found near steeply shelving beaches.

ATTACKS

Whilst many recorded shark attacks are preceded by exploratory nudges and bumps, great whites commonly take a far more direct approach. Strikes most often occur with great violence and suddenness. Far from the patrolling fins common in shark movies, or the relentless hunting depicted in *Jaws*, most great white strikes occur when the victim had little or no warning that the attacker was even in the area.

Wounds sustained in great white attacks are usually massive, with considerable loss of flesh. Great whites, too, are one of very few species credited with devouring human victims whole. Yet paradoxically, they often also seem to lose interest after the first bite.

Many survivors of encounters with great whites speak of the 'curiosity' of

COLOUR VARIATION

Although the dominant colour of the great white can be blue, grey, brown or even green, the underside is always pure white.

the would-be assailant. Divers, especially, report many incidents of being 'investigated' by curious great whites which made no attempt to attack. Surface bathers could easily be the subject of such investigation yet remain oblivious to it.

A particularly harrowing 'investigation' occurred as recently as July 1991 when an Italian woman was thrown from her canoe by a charge from a great white. The shark subsequently fol-

Left: A great white explores a metal cage. Above: 'Topside baiting' is used to attract this great white to the surface.

lowed her, at very close quarters, for some distance, but made no further attempt to strike.

Great whites, in common with several other species, seem especially drawn by spearfishing, perhaps attracted by the distress of injured fish. Although it is difficult to regard such a ferocious predator as a sneak thief, they have been known to 'steal' catches whilst making no attempt to harm the spearfisherman himself.

Floating objects of all kinds seem also to arouse their attention. Violent unprovoked strikes have been recorded on 'victims' as diverse as surfboards, research platforms, boats and even blocks of poly-

styrene. Boats have sometimes been damaged severely, with a peculiar glut of such incidents occurring in False Bay, South Africa. In some instances the offending shark has even leapt into the boat, injuring its occupants. Perhaps *Jaws* wasn't so far-fetched after all.

Perhaps what is surprising, given the awesome capabilities of the great white, is the number of victims – the majority – who do escape with their lives. A typical scenario might see the beast make a strong initial attack, then retire – perhaps to allow the victim to die from blood loss, thus avoiding any retaliatory danger to itself. In relatively few cases do great whites devour the human they attack, although they certainly possess the capacity to do so.

There is no doubt that the appetite of a large great white is prodigious.

BLUE POINTER, WHITE DEATH

The great white's scientific name is *Carcharodon carcharias*, although it is usually referred to by several other local titles: white, white death, white pointer (Australia), blue pointer (South Africa), and, simply, man-eater.

One captured off California, a 'mere' five metres (16½ft) in length, contained the bodies of two entire sea lions with a combined weight of over 135kg (298lbs). Another great white, a relatively small 900kg (1984lbs) specimen taken near Nagasaki, held the body of a 13 year-old boy.

JAWS – FACT IMITATING FICTION

Although the obsessive sea monster portrayed in Peter Benchley's notorious book is pure fiction, a not entirely dissimilar series of 'rogue shark' incidents occurred in much the same area during the summer of 1916. At Beach Haven, New Jersey, on 2 July, a 24 year old swimmer, Charles VanZant, was attacked in about 1.5 metres (5ft) of water whilst returning to shore. He died shortly later from shock and blood loss.

Four days later 28 year-old Charles Pruder was swimming some distance from shore at Spring Lake, 70km (44 miles) north of Beach Haven, when suddenly he disappeared from sight. Although he shortly died from bites which removed his left lower leg and part of his right abdomen, he was able to tell lifeguards that his assailant had been a shark.

Six days later still an even more horrific episode occurred in Matawan Creek, a narrow tidal waterway some 40km (25 miles) from Spring Lake. A long and confused sequence of events began to unroll when a group of men on a bridge noticed a long dark shadow heading upstream on the incoming tide – an uncanny echo of a scene from *Jaws*. Some time later a shark took 12 year-old Lester Stilwell, one of a group of boys using the creek to cool off on a summer's day.

Chaos ensued, with people fleeing the creek in panic, would-be rescuers trying to help, and men even trying to erect a barrier to prevent the attacker's escape. One Charles Fisher dived into the water, only to reappear in obvious distress holding, according to some accounts, his severed right leg. He died later in hospital. It later emerged that one of another group of bathers had been attacked some distance downstream whilst trying to flee the creek. Joseph Dunn sustained serious leg injuries, having evidently been pulled from a shark's jaws by friends.

What followed was a bout of shark hysteria not unlike that of 'Jaws'. Several sharks were killed and landed. The stomach of one of these, a 2.6 metre (8½ft) fish described as a great white caught 6 km (4 miles) from the mouth of the creek, contained 7kg (15lbs) of human remains, including the shinbone of a boy. It has since been speculated that the offending shark may in fact have been a bull shark, a creature with similar tooth-form and a more likely visitor to coastal creeks.

Despite the outwardly calm appearance of a patrolling great white (below left) they have the ability to suddenly strike their prey with frightening violence. Their sheer power, combined with chillingly efficient jaws (below), ensures that a victim receives massive wounds.

FOSSIL TEETH

Since all shark skeletons are composed of cartilage rather than bone, fossil remains are rare. However, fossil teeth identical in form to the modern great white's date back at least 60 million years to the Paleocene period. The largest of these are attributed to a 'giant' great white, *Carcharodon megalodon*, and measure over 15cm (6in) in length. It is estimated that their original host would have been over 16 metres (52½ft) long and weighed 20 tonnes/tons.

Anatomy of a Killer

IT IS a tribute to evolution's arrow that the modern shark is probably what a marine engineer would create if asked to create the fastest, most powerful underwater predator his imagination could design.

Although it varies considerably from species to species, the general body form of the shark is unmistakable. The streamlined body is flattened front and rear to minimise drag when turning and when undulating that striking tail fin. The tail fin itself is pronounced, particularly its upper lobe, for powerful swimming. The snout is elongated, with a wide, underhung jaw. The dorsal fin, with which killer sharks have announced their presence in a hundred movies, is strikingly triangular and erect.

SWIMMING

Even a still photograph of a shark is a chilling image of grace and power. In this case, beauty surely *is* the beast. Sharks swim with a sinuous motion as their powerful muscles send waves rippling along their bodies, with the bulk of the thrust coming from the tail. When 'cruising', typically at around one or two mph, the effect is almost languid. But sharks are also capable of frenzied bursts of activity and high speeds. Actual figures are disputed, but estimates of sharks' top speed range from 20 to well over 40mph.

BUOYANCY

Sharks control their depth by two means. When swimming, they use the angle of their pectoral fins much like a submarine's to 'fly' up or down. The bizarre head of the hammerhead shark is thought to operate as an 'extra fin' in this way, as well as housing even more

highly developed smell and electroreceptive organs than usual.

Unlike bony fishes, sharks possess no swim bladder to vary their buoyancy. Instead, they evolved a 'lightweight' construction which requires less effort to maintain their position in the water. As well as relatively light body tissues and a large, oily liver, shark skeletons are composed of cartilage (like your breastbone) – lighter, and more elastic than bone. Bottom-dwelling sharks, for obvious reasons, tend to be more dense than mid-water swimmers.

MUSCLEPOWER

Shark muscle is also comparatively light in weight. There are two types. In most species red muscle lies in a thin layer just beneath the skin. Like our muscles, this has a generous blood supply. It accounts for around one tenth of total muscle bulk and is used when the shark is cruising.

By far the largest muscle type is white muscle, the 'afterburner' used for sprint speeds. This type of tissue is very poorly supplied with blood vessels, and thus its endurance is short. Most species of shark quickly become exhausted by fast swimming.

ARMOUR

The skin of a shark, commonly used for shoes and handbags, is the organ most familiar in everyday life. In its natural form, its strong, rough surface is often described as 'sandpaper-like', which is hardly surprising: the skin is actually composed of highly evolved teeth or 'dermal denticles' which comprise a sort of flexible armour. Abrasion by shark skin can cause painful injuries. Although coarse in texture, it has been suggested

Below: A lemon shark attacks a diver's flipper, causing an element of panic.

that the alignment of these 'teeth' actually encourages water flow over the shark's body, and is even hydrodynamically 'quiet' – an obvious advantage to a hunting fish eager to keep its presence undetected.

Sharks, like all other fish, are cold blooded – their body temperature is close to that of their surroundings, rather than constant as in the case of warm-blooded animals such as mammals. However mackerel sharks (including the mako and great white), maintain a body temperature 5 to 11°C (8-20°F) higher than their surroundings. Although this does not make them strictly warm blooded, it allows greater muscle efficiency, as befits one of the more active families of shark. Some species of thresher shark show similar adaptations of body temperature.

RESPIRATION

A fish breathes by passing water through its mouth, over its gills and out again through gill slits. The gills are the equivalent of our lungs, extracting life-giving oxygen from the water which flows over them.

It used to be thought that if a shark ever stopped swimming, it would suffocate as the flow of oxygenated water over its gills would cease. In fact there are two broad types of gill structure. Some species, such as the mackerel sharks, rely on 'ram-jet' breathing and must indeed keep swimming to survive. Others, mainly sluggish bottom-dwellers, employ rhythmically contracting muscles to pump water over the gills. A few species, like the grey nurse, are capable of both methods of 'breathing'.

GROWTH

Compared to predatory bony fish, sharks are slow-growing, typically increasing by 15cm (6in) per year, but as little as 4cm (1¹/₂in). Longer-lived varieties, such as the piked dogfish, tend to grow slowest, and have been known to live for as long as 70 years, possibly 100. White, blue, mako and other large pelagic sharks are thought to be amongst the fastest growers, putting on some 30cm (1ft) per year.

REPRODUCTION

Despite the great age of shark species, their method of reproduction is considerably more sophisticated than that of most other fish. Bony fish tend to spawn huge numbers of tiny eggs which are fertilized externally and then

(in most cases) left to get on with it. This strategy offers a very low survival rate, compensated by the sheer number of eggs involved.

Sharks adopt two approaches, both of which result in fewer, better-developed young. Some 'oviparous' species lay large, well-protected eggs, sometimes found on seashores where they are commonly dubbed 'mermaid's purses'. Thus protected, the embryo shark can reach a degree of self-sufficiency before hatching.

In other species the developing egg is retained in the mother's body prior to hatching, allowing even greater security. The young produced by this 'ovoviviparous' method are born live and free-swimming. In a further refinement of ovoviviparous breeding, the developing

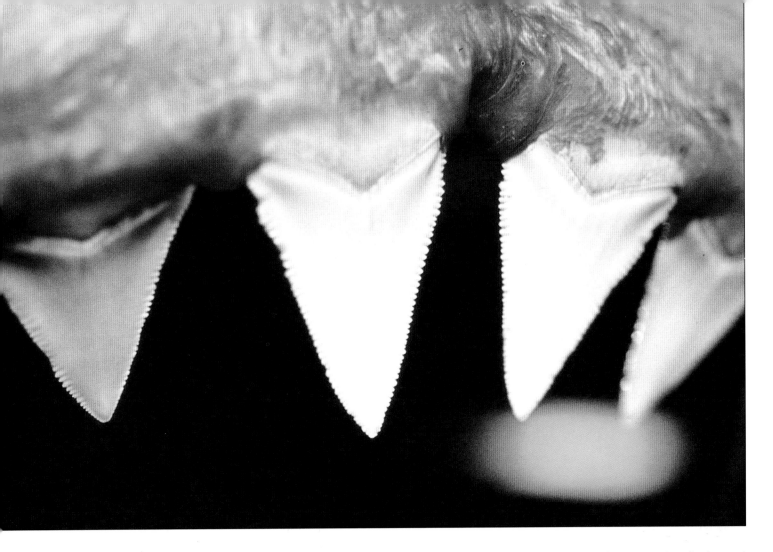

The torpedo shaped snout of a great white (left) is packed with sensory aids to guide the razor-sharp teeth (above).

sharks actually receive nutrients in the mother shark's uterus – a primitive form of the method adopted by mammals.

A grotesque variation on this approach is found in several species, including the mako, thresher and white, in which developing embryos feed off successive 'generations' of eggs which the mother releases, evidently for this precise purpose. Such uterine cannibalism is known as 'oophagy'. Litter sizes by these methods vary from two to over 100.

JAWS

Not surprisingly, sharks have a highly developed ability to bite things, but there is much more to this than an impressive array of teeth. In most species, the teeth are not in the ideal place for a hunter, but underslung and shrouded by a massive snout. The snout itself is vital, being crowded with sensory apparatus on which the predator shark relies.

However, in most species of shark, not only the lower jaw (as in humans) but the upper jaw, too, is separate from the skull. This forms a highly mobile structure which allows an attacking shark to tilt its head back, elongate its jaws and strike, usually with the lower teeth first. The force of a shark's bite can be so great that some have evolved an elaborate system of shock-absorbers to protect other vital organs from the impact.

One of the keys to the shark's success is its teeth. This is not simply a matter of their number, sharpness and ferocity, but the animal's ability to continually replace them throughout its life. You are very unlikely to encounter an unarmed shark.

Rather than being attached directly to its jaw, a shark's teeth are set, instead, in a membrane known as the tooth bed. New teeth are continually formed in grooves in this area, moving forward and maturing as the old teeth are lost or wear out. Replacement occurs every one to two weeks. Often more than one tooth on the same row is ready for action, giving the shark's jaws the disquieting effect of a nest of circular saws.

Individual teeth vary widely in size, number and form. Some are small, almost delicate, and too numerous to count. Others, such as the great white's, are large, sturdy and serrated. To a large extent these differences reflect the diet of the species concerned. Far from being the indifferent dustbins of the underwater world, most shark species are highly specialized feeders, occupying a particular ecological niche just like their counterparts on land. But for a few, a human leg dangled in the water is close enough to the usual quarry to be worth at least an exploratory bite . . .

Shark Senses

ONE OF the characteristics which distinguish plants and animals is the latter's capacity for sensing its surroundings, and responding to its findings in some coherent way. And if the range and acuteness of these senses signifies an animal's state of development, then the shark is a very sophisticated organism indeed.

We humans normally think of five senses: sight, smell, hearing, touch and taste, with smell and taste being closely related. Sharks are even better equipped.

SMELL AND TASTE

Fishermen have long known of the acuity of the shark's sense of smell. For centuries (as well as in *Jaws*), the preferred method of attracting sharks has been to lace the water with chum (chopped bait and blood). In laboratory tests, constituents of blood and meat cause a great increase in electrical activity in sharks' olfactory centres. At sea, such chemicals aroused characteristic hunting patterns, either criss-crossing an area or homing-in on the source of the smell. High concentrations can put sharks into an attacking frenzy, biting at anything they see – even streams of air bubbles. Clearly, smell plays a crucial role in arousing the shark's instinct to attack.

Sharks' sense of taste, too, is well developed, but thought generally to be used by the animal in deciding whether to accept or reject something already bitten. By this time, the distinction is probably lost on the victim. Early methods of deterring attack, dealt with in detail on pages 76 to 81, naturally focused on the shark's sense of taste and smell.

TOUCH AND 'SUPER TOUCH'

As well as the sense of touch with which we are familiar, the shark possesses a highly developed faculty which falls somewhere between touch and hearing. Situated along the shark's body in a region called the lateral line are series of shallow pits and grooves housing highly specialised cells with hair-like projections. These hairs, or *cilia*, respond to minute pressure changes in the water, and can pick up both the magnitude and direction of the movements of another fish (or bather).

A sophisticated feedback system prevents the shark's own movements from interfering with the incoming signal, which allows the shark to detect possible prey a great distance in even the murkiest of water. Clearly the more distressed a potential victim might be, whether through injury, drowning or even water games, the more violent these signals will be.

HEARING

The shark's sense of hearing is closely related to its lateral line, and appears to comprise a concentration of similar cells in the inner ear. Again, it is thought to be particularly sensitive to low-pitched vibrations, such as might be made by a struggling fish.

Below: This diagram indicates the main senses that sharks have at their disposal to identify a source of food and home-in on it with precision.

Right: Sharks use their full complement of senses to locate their prey, and often round-up shoals of fish before beginning to feed on them.

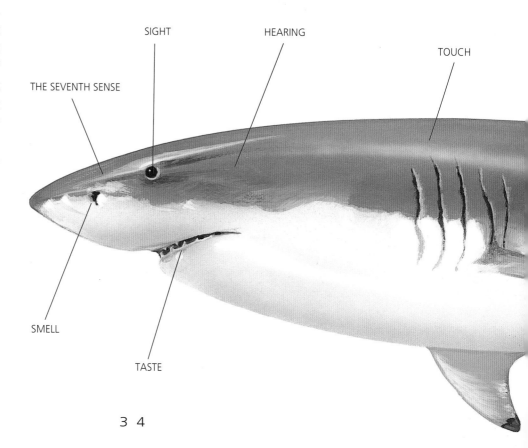

SIGHT

HEARING

TOUCH

THE SEVENTH SENSE

SMELL

TASTE

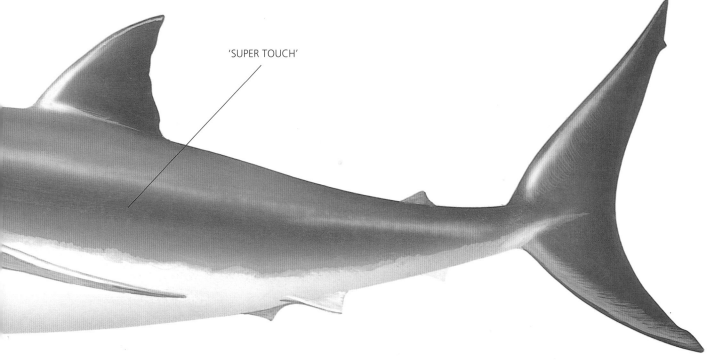

'SUPER TOUCH'

VISION

Those cold, cruel eyes represent what is probably the least impressive of the shark's repertoire of senses. Sharks don't see too well, and the construction of most species' eyes is biased towards performing best in dim conditions. But the species with the best developed eyes tend to be those active, fast-moving varieties which are most likely to attack man. Most have no movable eyelids, although certain *carcharhinid* sharks such as the great white have a

Left: A great white displays its teeth.
Below: The cold, cruel eye of a blue shark.

retractable membrane which protects the eye during attacks.

THE SEVENTH SENSE

Perhaps the most intriguing of the shark's senses is electromagnetic – a system so sensitive that perhaps sharks don't need to see at all. Although this faculty is by no means fully understood, sharks are able to detect both minute voltage changes in their surroundings, and magnetic variations, by means of a network of electro-receptors (the *ampullae of Lorenzini*) in the head.

Experiments suggest that sharks use this ability like an in-built compass, in order to navigate as they prowl the oceans. It is also apparent that they can detect the minute electrical impulses emitted by other animals, even enabling them to locate creatures buried in the sea-bed.

Of all these senses, it is believed that smell, movement detection and electro-location are the most fundamental to a hunting shark. The first two enable a stalking shark to locate and home in on potential prey from great distance. As the target closes, the electro-receptors come increasingly into play. Sharks can 'see' their victims in ways which we can scarcely imagine.

Attack Methods

EVEN A cursory reading of the preceding chapter ought to show what a sophisticated hunter the predatory shark can be. As well as its awesome physical adaptation, the shark houses sensory apparatus which any nuclear submarine captain might be proud to have at his disposal.

A shark's sense of smell is, in certain species, capable of distinguishing chemicals in concentrations as low as one part per million. As well as allowing a shark to detect potential prey, such capabilities are believed to play a part in species recognition and mating behaviour. As we have seen, most dangerous sharks also possess excellent vision, hearing, plus 'extra' senses for detecting minute electrical impulses and vibration.

Add this to a strong-swimming, powerful body and a powerful set of teeth and jaws, and it is little wonder that the shark is such an unparalleled underwater predator. There are very few large creatures in the sea that a shark cannot detect and, once detected, inflict immense harm upon.

Research on individuals in captivity has also shown that, far from being primitive and instinctive eating machines, sharks also display some signs of higher intelligence. Sharks can certainly learn from their actions. Their ratio of brain mass to overall body mass is comparable with the 'brainier' birds and even some mammals. On the whole, younger sharks are more active, inquisitive and aggressive than more experienced mature specimens. This is perhaps some

reassurance, as younger sharks are, on the whole, smaller.

It is thought that a prowling shark uses its sense of smell and its movement detectors to close in on potential prey. As the shark draws near its victim, sight and electro-sensors take over, in preparation for the final strike.

THE STRIKE

It used to be thought that sharks had to roll onto their side to bring their underhung jaws into the attack position, but this is clearly not the case. In the modern shark, the jaw is quite separate from the skull. Most species have the capacity to elevate the snout and upper jaw, and charge head-on to confront their hapless victim with nothing but rows of lethal teeth.

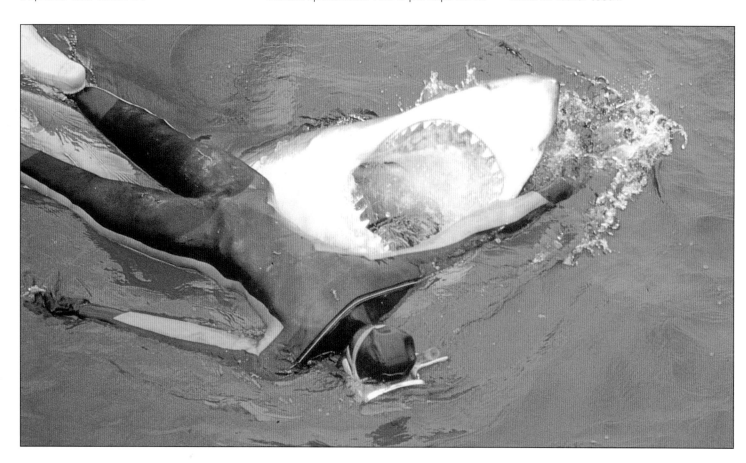

A great white shark attacks a dummy diver (below left) and seizes the model in an explosion of foam (above).

Most species which are known to be dangerous to man have lower jaws housing sharply-pointed spike-like teeth. These are inserted into the victim first, after which the upper jaw protrudes and strikes. The teeth in this jaw are usually flatter and more serrated. The typical bite is more of a sawing action than a simple bite: the lower teeth grip whilst a lashing motion of the head and body causes the serrated upper teeth to sheer through flesh like a band saw. Such a shark's sideways threshing motion may look frenzied, but it is completely purposeful.

Often, an 'exploratory' strike precedes a full attack, or may take its place altogether. It was once believed that most, if not all, shark attacks on humans were motivated by the straight-forward desire to feed. Experts now believe that the majority arise from some other cause. This is partly because so many victims survive and partly because the risk of attack appears to increase when visibility is poor, suggesting that many so-called attacks are really exploratory physical examinations.

Such nudges can, however, be both violent in themselves and the prelude to

something more violent still. On Christmas Eve 1960, Petrus Sithole was swimming in about 2 metres (6½ft) of water, 60 metres (200ft) from shore at Margate Beach, South Africa. Suddenly the unfortunate Sithole screamed as he was lifted forcefully out of the water by a blow from what turned out to be a Zambezi (bull) shark. As he fell back into the water, the shark severed both his legs. He was dead before he could be recovered from the water.

Although most attacks on humans come from below, this is only to be expected as victims are usually on or close to the surface when struck. In deep water, sharks can and will attack from any angle. The widespread notion that sharks commonly circle their victim (usually displaying the tell-tale triangular dorsal fin), is largely false. Only in some seven per cent of attacks are sharks first seen circling their victims. Such instances appear more common when involving pelagic sharks, such as the blue, in oceanic waters.

Far from making visual threats, in the majority of cases studied – perhaps two-thirds – the shark was not seen at all by its victim prior to the instant of attack. In strikes on divers, this ratio inevitably falls, as he is better placed

and motivated to observe his surroundings. Some species of shark are known to exhibit tell-tale 'body language' when threatened, startled or aggressive, and experienced divers learn to interpret this and take extra care.

Equally, the nightmare scenario of frenzied mass attacks by groups of sharks is the exception, accounting for perhaps one out of every 20 recorded cases. However, the equally common notion that erratic splashing movements may encourage an attack appears to have some foundation. Such actions have been shown in experiments to arouse some shark species to aggressive behaviour, perhaps through mimicking the behaviour of distressed fish.

The 'typical' attack is, therefore, by a solitary animal, close to shore, in conditions of poor underwater visibility. It may be preceded by an 'exploratory' bump of varying severity. It will probably comprise few actual attacking bites – commonly as few as one – and other people in the water are unlikely to be directly threatened. It will probably be survivable, given prompt medical attention. However, reassuring though these findings might be, there are a great many documented exceptions to each of them.

APPETITE

Most sharks are active creatures which need a substantial diet to provide them with the necessary raw materials for energy, growth and reproduction. Firm figures are inevitably hard to come by, but it appears that sharks need to eat food equivalent to something between 1.5 and 3 per cent of its bodyweight per day. For a 1 tonne/ton large great white, this equates to between 5.5 and 11 tonnes/tons of food per year – a prodigious sum.

Although active sharks are thought to need to eat every two days or so, they can survive without food for very much longer. In captivity they have been observed to fast for several months. During such periods, the body sustains itself on reserves of nutrients located in the liver.

Shark Attacks – a Global Overview

PERHAPS the most compelling 'fact' about sharks, is how little we really know about them. Except when they bite a hook or a man, or attract the attention of nature programme makers, their lives are generally shrouded in a mystery which only adds to their chilling aura of menace.

Much of our information about shark attack is really little more than a reflection of human behaviour. Most shark attacks occur in calm water in fine weather. Most occur at weekends. Most occur in waist-deep water. Most occur between latitudes 47 degrees South and 46 degrees North (Southern New Zealand, say, to Bordeaux). But these are precisely the conditions and places where people are more often found in the sea: it is inconceivable, for instance, that most sharks are 'off-duty' from Monday to Friday. Sharks are found – and undoubtedly feed – in all the oceans. It is we that are the variable, just as we are the intruder on their domain.

It is probably true, too, that even our knowledge of sharks' most direct encounters with man – attacks on human beings – is incomplete. Much of the accurately recorded information about human casualties comes from the developed world: Europe, North America, Australasia and South Africa. Even allowing for the far higher incidence of water sports in such regions, it is unlikely that sharks are any less voracious elsewhere. Poor Indians bathing in the Ganges, and subsistence fishermen off the African coast, must surely face at least as great a risk. It is simply that for most of this century nobody has taken the trouble to record it systematically.

Although the ultimate horror of shark attack is being eaten alive, the

Below: Nobody who faces a great white at close range can doubt its danger.

majority of victims suffer no such fate. Most attacks comprise one or two strikes, with a similar number of bites or slashes. Sometimes it is difficult not to view the author of such attacks as merely opportunist, probing or perhaps mildly irritable.

Such thoughts must have been a long way from the mind of the commercial fisherman who hooked a 400kg (882lbs) tiger shark 32km (20 miles) off Venice, Florida, in March 1944. Inside he was horrified to find the body of a man, almost whole from the third rib down to the knees.

Yet attacks in which the shark seemed determined to kill his victim are relatively rare, and the wild frenzied attack of legend even more so – perhaps one in 20. For all their chilling efficiency, many of their attacks seem relatively half-hearted, almost casual, affairs. Sharks allow their victims to escape with their lives something like 80 per cent of the time. Perhaps they don't like the taste.

And the attacks themselves are, of course, rare. There are no accurate global figures, but estimates put the number of world-wide fatalities at no more than 20 per year – about the same number as are killed annually by bee and wasp stings in the USA alone; rather less than the number of people who will make a major killing next year on the British national lottery. In the waters off Australia, the world's shark attack capital, drownings outnumber shark attacks by some 50:1, with most of those attacks non-fatal. In South Africa the ratio is believed to be around 600:1; in the USA, as high as 1000:1.

Nor is it just very large sharks which are dangerous. Any shark over 2 metres (6¹/₂ft) in length can launch a potentially fatal attack. The species known to be most dangerous are considered in more detail on pages 18 to 29, but it is prudent to regard any but the smallest sharks as potentially dangerous.

Sharks are never 'off-duty', and size is not always important when it comes to an attack. The great white (above) is always dangerous, but a grey reef shark (below) can also inflict serious injury.

LOCATION OF ATTACKS

Information from the US Navy International Shark Attack File, based on over 1600 cases.

AFRICA 123
(South Africa 99, Mozambique 10)

AMERICA, NORTH 225
(Florida 107, California 46, South Carolina 23, New Jersey 17)

AMERICA, SOUTH 8

AMERICA, CENTRAL 47
(Mexico 28)

ASIA
Indian Ocean 34
(Iran 17)
Pacific Ocean 49
(Philippines 18)
Red Sea 3

AUSTRALIA 309
(New South Wales 137, Queensland 57, Torres Straight 43)

EUROPE 33
(Yugoslavia 12)

NEW GUINEA 53

NEW ZEALAND 29

OCEANIC ISLANDS
Atlantic Ocean 7
(Bermuda 6)
Indian Ocean 4
Pacific Ocean 137
(Hawaii 31, Bismark Archipelago 28, Fiji Islands 22, Solomon Islands 19)

WEST INDIES 55
(Cuba 15, Bahamas 11)

LARGEST ROD-CAUGHT

Officially, the largest fish ever caught on a rod is a 1208kg (1¼ tons) great white shark landed by Alf Dean at Denial Bay near Ceduna, South Australia on 21 April 1959. This monster was 5.13 metres (16ft 10in) long. An even larger great white, scaling 1537kg (1½ tons), was hooked in 1976 off Albany, Western Australia, but the catch was not ratified as whale meat was used as bait.

ROD-CAUGHT RECORDS, BY SPECIES:

Hammerhead, 449.5kg (991lbs), Sarasota, Florida, 1982
Mako, 489.88kg (1080lbs), Montauk, New York, 1979
Porbeagle, 210.92kg (465lbs), Cornwall, England, 1976
Thresher, 363.8kg (802lbs), Tutukaka, New Zealand, 1981
Tiger, 807.4kg (1780lbs), Cherry Grove, South Carolina, 1964
Great white, 1208.38kg (1¼ tons), Ceduna, South Australia, 1959

ATTACKS: DESCRIPTION OF LOCALITY	
Close to shore/beach	44%
Offshore bar/reef/bank	20%
Harbour/bay	9%
Open Sea	9%
River, other than mouth	7%
Alongside jetty/dock/breakwater	4%
Mouth of river/creek	2%
Others	4%

ATTACKS: OUTCOME	
Non-fatal	65%
Fatal	31%
Assumed fatal	4%

ATTACKS: DESCRIPTION OF INJURIES	
Calf/Knee	40%
Thigh	33%
Arms	23%

DESCRIPTION OF INJURIES Continued	
Feet	18%
Hands	15%
Buttocks	10%
Fingers/toes	10%
Abdomen/stomach	8%
Chest	6%
Shoulder	4%
Back	4%
Head	2%

Left: Great white sharks often enter shallow water, putting them in close proximity to bathers and surfers.

Below left: Deep sea fishing for sharks is a specialized sport, but even British waters could hold a record-breaker.

Below: The major shark attack areas are well documented, and reflect human activities in the world's oceans.

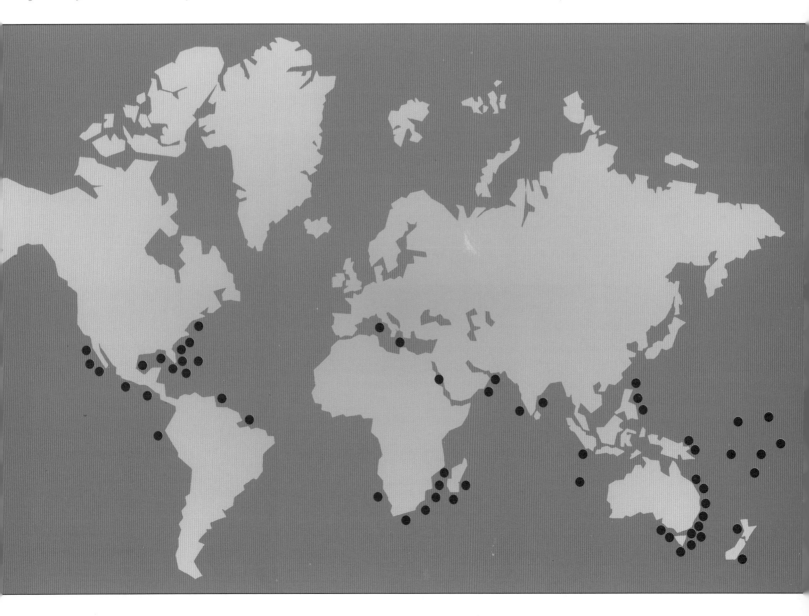

GROUP ATTACKS

Although the vast majority of attacks concern a lone shark attacking a single bather – even when there are other bathers close by – this is certainly not always the case. On 27 March 1937 Norman Girvan was one of three men swimming ashore from a sandbank across a 200 metre (650ft) channel, when he was suddenly and violently attacked. A companion described his arm raised in alarm and 'blood shooting everywhere'. Girvan was able to say 'It won't let go, it's got my leg'.

The other swimmer, Jack Brinkley, attempted to assist but was himself attacked. Although rescued, he died later of severe wounds to his left side and arm, the latter being almost severed. One day later a 3.5 metre (11½ft) tiger shark was caught nearby. It's stomach was found to contain legs and arms identified as Girvan's. His torso was later washed ashore.

NATURAL ENEMIES

It was once thought that the presence of dolphins or porpoises – natural enemies of the shark – conferred some degree of safety upon humans bathing in the same area. However, on 19 March 1967, near Paradise Beach, Natal, South Africa, Len Jones was spearfishing when events proved this supposition to be wrong. Jones was at the surface with two dead fish attached to his belt when he was suddenly thrown clear of the water by a charge from a shark, which shook him violently.

Astonishingly, the diver was able to persuade the shark to release him by punching and pushing it with both hands. It continued to circle him for some time but did not resume the attack. Jones was extremely lucky to escape with only minor injuries.

Although attacks occur in an almost infinite variety of circumstances, it is possible to identify some factors which appear more likely to precede strikes on humans. If there is such a thing as a 'typical' incident, it occurs in murky water close to shore, but adjacent to deeper water. There will usually be only one victim, who is more likely to be a lone swimmer than a member of a group. There is some suggestion that uneven tanning is also a risk factor.

Neither a bleeding wound nor menstruation has been shown to have a bearing, but it would be wise not to take the risk. Equally, the well-known caution about bathers physically attracting attention to themselves is unproven, but probably well worth taking on board. Laboratory tests suggest that erratic splashing movements can stimulate aggressive behaviour in sharks.

Below: A tiger shark in shallow water.

History of Attacks

MAN'S fascination with monsters – real and imagined – is probably as old as man himself. Although modern man is far more likely than his forebears to venture into the shark's domain, this beautiful, terrible creature has fascinated observers for centuries.

In the chapter devoted to myths (page 86), we will look more closely at some of the more mystical beliefs and attitudes that sharks have engendered over the centuries – and continue to arouse. Although archeological evidence shows that man was a fisherman well into the stone age, and presumably came into contact with sharks, history has, perhaps inevitably, been far more sparing with shark facts.

Other than from fossil evidence, much of 'shark history' shares the same homocentric problem which accompanies contemporary anecdotes about shark attacks. For it is not truly an account of shark behaviour at all, so much as a version of man's ability to record it. Inevitably, such early accounts focus on the eastern Mediterranean, the so-called 'cradle of civilisation', where people had the time and inclination to jot things down for posterity. And, from time to time, the cradle was indeed rocked by you-know-what.

Evidence from ancient Malta suggests that sharks – and more specifically the great white – were objects of fear as early as 2000BC. The ancient Greeks, too, learned to fear what they called 'lamia', a name that meant both a fabulous monster and a voracious fish. Steven Speilberg may not have known it, but in making the film *Jaws*, he was in part re-enacting the fantasies of classical Greece.

The Greek historian Herodotus (485-425BC) was a great traveller throughout much of the Mediterranean. He described a great battle between the ancient Greek and Persian fleets near the Headlands of Athos in north-eastern Greece, in which a great number of Persian sailors were taken and devoured by 'lamia'.

A Greek tragic poem from the same period also records an event familiar today, that of a sponge diver attacked as he climbed back into his boat. In this instance, the diver lost both legs. Some centuries later in 77AD, Pliny the Elder describes sponge divers engaged in 'fierce fights with dog-fish'.

Above: Sharks attack shipwrecked sailors in this picture from 'Le Petit Parisien', 1901.

It has even been suggested that the 'whale' which swallowed Jonah was in fact a great white. In the original Hebrew version the beast involved was not specifically a whale, but merely some variety of large marine animal.

Most of this early evidence is fragmented and vague, although the 16th Century French naturalist Guillame Rondelet describes the recovery of human bodies, whole and fully clothed, from the stomachs of what, by his description, were probably great white sharks. Sadly M. Rondelet's accounts are robbed of credibility by his assertion that at least one of the bodies in question was clothed in armour.

It was not until the advent of mass communication – and perhaps the vicarious pleasures it encouraged – that accounts of shark attacks fell fully into the public domain.

Le Petit Parisien, a French magazine popular at the turn of the century, often featured gory accounts of shark attack: a Tunisian sponge diver who lost a leg; four female bathers attacked, one fatally, off Trieste; and, most grotesque of all, the body of a man, woman and child recovered from the belly of a great white off Sicily.

Even as late as World War One, a series of attacks on America's Atlantic seaboard provoked a feeding frenzy – amongst newspapers – which threatened to dislodge the Battle of the Somme from the front pages. Such accounts, which might as easily be found in today's more sensational Sunday newspapers, truly bring us to the modern era. Only the sharks themselves remain unchanged.

Right: Sharks attack the crew of a shipwreck in the Pacific ocean, as depicted on the front cover of 'Le Petit Parisien' in 1906. This popular French magazine often featured colourful accounts of shark attacks.

'SHOCKING' LANGUAGE

Even the derivation of the word 'shark' is unclear. To the ancient Greeks, sharks were *lamia*, along with anything else big and ferocious that lurked in the depths. In the 16th century, the word *tiburon*, probably of Spanish or Portuguese origin, was generally applied. The bonnet shark, *Sphyrna tiburo*, retains a relic of that name.

The modern word 'shark' possibly arrived in 1569 when Sir John Hawkin's Caribbean expedition brought such an exhibit back to London. This may have been a corruption of a Mayan hieroglyph, xoc (pronounced 'shock'), depicting a fish. Certainly Shakespeare was able to use the word in Hamlet in 1602.

Attacks: Australia

AUSTRALIA can legitimately claim the unwelcome distinction of being the shark attack capital of the world. Almost two centuries ago, with colonial Australia itself but a few decades old, the shark attack threat was already common currency. The first known newspaper warning about a dangerous shark in Sydney Harbour dates from as early as 1806.

By the early years of the 20th Century, Australia was beginning to take sharks more seriously, with a more systematic attempt at record-keeping. In 1912, again in the broad waters of Sydney Harbour, a shark described as a 'whaler' seized a man, taking part of his thigh and genitalia.

Below: The famous Great Barrier Reef, Australia, as viewed from the air.

In June 1923, near Bellambi Reef, New South Wales, four fishermen found their boat capsized from under them by a shark, which later took one of the men, Two of the others were presumed to have drowned, leaving only one survivor. In the following decade at least two other attacks on boats were recorded.

Four attacks spaced through one decade, all in the Sydney Harbour area, illustrate how close inshore sharks are prepared to strike, and even how close to urban areas. In 1919 a boy received horrific and fatal leg injuries as he waded out for an early morning swim. His thigh bone was exposed and its major artery severed.

Right: Lifesavers plough their boat into the surf off the Sydney coastline.

Five years later, also in January, another youth was fatally bitten in only 1 metre (3ft 4in) of water. Five years later still, yet another youth died in the same Parramatta River when a shark severed his left arm. Also in 1929, a 20 year old man was attacked in nearby Maroubra Bay. His injuries would certainly have been survivable today but he died of infection a week later.

Nor are large crowds and boats in the water any apparent deterrent. In 1930 a swimmer, Norman Clarke, was seized by a shark in the full view of a large gallery enjoying a yacht race in Port Philip Bay, Melbourne. The horrified audience watched as Clarke battled vainly with the shark before it swam out to sea with what was left of him.

As elsewhere, the majority of known Australian attacks take place in the summer months, in daylight, within 50 metres (165ft) of shore – no more than a reflection of people's bathing habits. Indeed, more detailed study reveals that in the extreme north of the country, where it is 'summer' all year round, there

are no seasonal highs or lows. Equally, attacks are concentrated on the eastern seaboard, notably around Sydney – the region of densest population.

In recent decades, the shark 'menace' has led to the widespread erection of shark nets and mesh defences near Australia's principal recreational beaches. The most common species caught in such nets are hammerheads.

BONDI HORROR

Bondi Beach, just a few miles from downtown Sydney, is one of Australia's best known and most popular bathing and surfing areas. Indeed, it is so famous that most people in Britain

Caution, do not mix! An Australian surfer (above) is well aware that a great white (below) may lurk in the water.

Above: Rodney Fox shows his scars.

seem to have heard of it. Regrettably, so have the sharks.

In one short period during the summer of 1929 two males died as a result of separate shark attacks. One, a youth, was seized in just 1.2 metres (4ft) of water by an unidentified shark. Although quickly rescued, he soon died from injuries, including a chunk of bone torn from his pelvis and massive tissue loss from his hip and thigh.

The second victim also survived the attack only to die in hospital. A shark had taken a bite measuring 38 x 18cm (1ft 2in x 7in) from his thigh, severing his femoral artery.

AUSTRALIA: KNOWN MAN-EATERS

Great white
Tiger shark
Copper shark (bronze whaler)
Bull shark (Zambezi shark)
Blue shark
Shortfin mako
Hammerheads, various

SURVIVORS

Rodney Fox should have been in no doubt that spearfishermen are indeed a high-risk group for shark attack. In 1961 his friend and spearfishing rival, Brian Rodger, was attacked by a great white shark off South Australia. He was lucky to escape with a grotesquely lacerated leg.

Two years later, in August 1963, Fox himself was competing in the South Australian spearfishing championship at Aldinga Beach near Adelaide, when he had an even more terrifying encounter with a great white shark. The water was murky so Fox had little warning when the monster fastened its jaws in a vice-like grip around his chest and arm.

Fox attempted to prod the shark in the eye with his free right hand, only for it to slip into the shark's mouth, where it was lacerated down to the bone. Miraculously, despite injuries which left his ribs and viscera horribly exposed and one lung punctured, Fox was able to escape to a nearby boat. He was rushed to hospital where it took no less than 462 stitches to put him back together during a four hour operation.

Just as horrifying, but amusing in its black way, was the case of another diver, Henri Bource, who in 1964 lost a leg in a shark attack off Lady Julia Percy Island, Victoria. Four years later the hapless Bource lost a second leg in yet another shark attack. Fortunately for him, it was his artificial one.

Above: Bondi Beach, famous for its bathing and surfing – and its shark attacks!

Attacks: North America

ALTHOUGH shark attacks have been reported over almost every stretch of US coastline, the chief danger zones are California and Florida. Not surprisingly, both host well-known holiday and water sports resorts where large urban populations live close to the sea. Perhaps more particularly, as well as normal bathing activities, scuba diving and snorkelling are common pursuits in both. Attacks on divers and other 'offshore' victims are especially common.

The two regions, however, host different types of killer. The colder waters of the western seaboard, particularly off northern California, witness a high frequency of incidents involving great white sharks. A second, but much smaller, great white hot spot occurs in New England – home to the fictional *Jaws*. Great white attacks are unknown in the warmer waters of the southern states and the Gulf of Mexico.

The most northerly shark attack in US Atlantic waters was the work of a great white. On 25th July 1936, at Buzzards Bay, Massachusetts, 16 year-old Joseph Troy was was attacked and dragged under by the shark. His companion valiantly went to his aid, and was able to support Troy until a boat arrived on the scene. The shark remained in the area but did not strike again. The unfortunate Troy later died in hospital whilst his leg was being amputated. Yet again, however, this demonstrates the apparent reluctance of sharks to press home an attack, or to divert their attention to rescuers even when there is ample opportunity to do so.

Florida, dangling as it does into the Caribbean, enjoys much warmer water temperatures than other US seas, with bathing possible all year round. By far the most prolific killer in such waters is the tiger shark. Attacks have also been recorded by hammerhead, bull, nurse and oceanic whitetip sharks.

Yet as late as the early thirties, eminent US shark experts continued to deny that sharks ever attacked human beings in American waters. The evidence which appeared to change their minds was an attack on a woman off Palm Beach, Florida on the first day of autumn 1931. The woman bather was struck by a fish which the lifeguard who went to her rescue was able to identify as a 2.4 metre (8ft) hammerhead shark. Despite severe damage to her right leg, there was no serious arterial harm and she made a full recovery.

Since that time the reality of shark attacks has been faced, and the USA has been at the forefront of research into sharks and their behaviour, both from military and civilian points of view.

Below: The cool waters of the California coastline witness a high proportion of the recorded great white shark attacks in North America.
Below right: It is suggested that divers wearing dark-coloured wet suits may be mistaken for seals, increasing the likelihood of 'mistaken identity' attacks.

THE HIGH PRICE OF ABALONE

In the 1970s great whites appeared to become increasingly common along the North Californian coast as conservation measures increased the population of sea lions, believed to be their principal prey. A corollary of this is the frequent suggestion that divers wearing dark-coloured wet suits might be mistaken for seals or sea lions, to their obvious peril. When this comes together with other 'risk factors', attacks might be expected to increase.

Bodega Bay, near Tomales Point, California, is a known shark attack 'hot spot', with three serious incidents in a four year period from 1968 to 1972. This is also a locality in which underwater visibility is poor, a feature often associated with attacks.

On 27th July 1968, Frank Logan was diving for abalone (a shellfish delicacy) off Bird Rock. He was at a depth of 6 metres (20ft) when he felt a bump. Turning to the source of this intrusion he was horrified to find himself in the mouth of a 6 metre (20ft) shark from his shoulders to his hip, being pushed sideways through the water. Logan then 'went limp', whereupon the shark let go of him.

It subsequently required over 200 stitches to close Logan's wounds. He was wearing a black wet-suit at the time. Although it has been suggested, in this and other attacks, that his attacker may thus have mistaken him for a seal, the rubber suit probably played a part in holding his torn body together. Logan's weighted diving belt was never recovered, and it has been speculated that this fell into the shark's throat and that in order to spit it out, the shark had first to release its prey. Logan later remarked, with chilling understatement, that 'I guess I'm pretty lucky.'

14 months after Logan's remarkable escape, Donald Joslin was diving in the same area when he felt a 'vice-like' pressure on his right leg and was pushed clear of the water. As he fell back, the impact appeared to wrench him free. The shark, a 5 metre (16½ft) great white, renewed its attack but Joslin beat it vigorously with his abalone iron and it moved away.

In late May 1972, another abalone diver, Helmut Himmrich, was struck on the leg by a 4 metre (13ft) shark as he was returning to his boat. Luckily his companions were able to haul him aboard, and he (and the leg) survived, despite severe tissue-loss from knee to buttock.

EATEN WHOLE

Perhaps the ultimate horror carried by any shark is the nightmare of its eating us whole. Yet, as we have seen, this is a rarity amongst documented cases. Indeed, from a rational standpoint, it might be the case that such a quick death is preferable to the lingering agony that often ensues.

Two cases from the fifties, from opposite sides of the continent, illustrate these extremes. In July 1952, 17 year-old Barry Wilson was swimming about 30 metres (100ft) offshore from Pacific Grove, California when he was attacked by a 3.6 metre (12ft) great white, thrown clear of the water then dragged under again. Rescuers managed to get Wilson onto an inflated inner tube, but the shark struck again and he was dead by the time he was brought ashore. Wilson's injuries were appalling, with both legs and one buttock virtually denuded of flesh.

Almost exactly seven years later, Robert Pamperin and a friend were diving for abalone some 50 metres (165ft) from shore at La Jolla Cove, California. Pamperin had just returned to the surface when, like Wilson, he was thrown clear of the water, and then pulled under by what was believed to be a tiger shark over 6 metres (20ft) in length. Pamperin's companion bravely dived to help, observing the shark lying on the sea bed with its victim waist-deep in its jaws and apparently dead. The shark resisted all attempts to distract it. Pamperin's body was never recovered, and he was presumed to have been eaten whole.

NORTH AMERICA: KNOWN MAN-EATERS

Tiger shark
Great white
Bull shark
Hammerhead sharks, various species
Lemon shark
Dusky shark
Blue shark
Oceanic whitetip shark

Possibles: sandbar shark, blacktip, Caribbean reef shark, spinner shark

Mako, porbeagle, threshers and salmon sharks are certainly big enough to kill humans, but there are no recorded unprovoked attacks.

Both pictures: A 'shark-proof' cage is the safest place to be when great whites such as these are feeling hungry.

Attacks: Pacific

SOME OF the oldest myths and legends about sharks originate from the vast Pacific region, and it would be surprising if the reality of shark attacks were not similarly widespread. Although this is almost certainly true, the remoteness of many of the ocean's islands means that much of what probably occurs goes unrecorded. With the exception, in modern times, of New Zealand and Hawaii, hard documentary evidence, is very piecemeal.

It seems likely that the shark was simply one more fact of life for the Pacific's native fishermen long before the phenomenon of shark attack was recognised in Europe. Although a high proportion of recorded incidents concerns recreational water users (especially spearfishermen), it is likely that unreported attacks on native islanders represent the unsung majority. Since the damage has already been done and nothing further can be gained, why bother to make it 'official'. The vast expanses of the Pacific, too, have been the scene of many of the most chilling mass attacks, a topic dealt with in more detail on page 66.

Shark researchers have postulated that most Pacific attacks can be divided between two distinct types of shark behaviour: 'feeding' attacks and 'aggressive' attacks, although the distinction might be lost on any victim. Aggressive attacks arise from the natural territorial behaviour of many shark species, not unlike the robin's assaults on anything red, or the dog defending its owner's home. Divers often report that such attacks are often associated with characteristic threat postures, such as head shaking or back arching. Many species of shark, including pelagic sharks and reef dwellers, display such behaviour.

Aggressive species such as great white and tiger sharks are the most common culprits in feeding attacks. Although the description might seem straightforward, there is some evidence that the sharks concerned strike through mistaking their victims for seals or turtles, believed to be their staple diet. The fact that great white attacks are restricted to the Hawaiian archipelago, the only Pacific area with a significant seal population, gives credence to this suggestion.

Many victims, whether surfers or divers, are clad in wet suits, which might easily cause them to be confused with seals, particularly when visibility is poor. The underside of a surfboard may equally be confused with a turtles belly. Indeed, surfboards themselves, or even chunks of polystyrene, are not immune from attack.

This highlights the truth underlying almost all shark attacks. The sea is their territory, not ours, and we venture into it at our peril. Indeed, given the awesome capability of a large shark, perhaps the wonder is that they let us off so lightly.

Above: This picture illustrates how
easily a shark might confuse the outline
of a surfer with that of a seal.
Below: Hanauma Bay, Oahu, Hawaii.
Below right: A big game fisherman lands
a large shark, Kona Coast, Hawaii.

UNLIKELY DETERRENTS

Several Pacific attacks illustrate the apparent, and surprising, reluctance of sharks to press home an attack. In many instances it seems that almost any reaction, feeble though it might seem when compared to the power of the shark, can deflect its intentions.

One of the most remarkable 'deterrents' on record was wielded by native fisherman Saburo Dooley off Palau in the Western Caroline Islands on the night of 4th November 1963. Dooley had been standing waist deep in the water for several hours, using a light to attract fish. His catch was tied to his body.

No sooner had Dooley turned off his light than he was bitten on the leg by a shark. Instinctively, he turned the light back on, shining it at his attacker, which just as quickly let go. Dooley was able to leave the water without further injury and made a full recovery.

The reaction of spearfisherman Bernard Moitessier was more conventional, but just as effective. He had caught, and then lost, a small shark when he felt himself attacked from behind by what turned out to be a much larger one, which had his right foot in its mouth. However, when Moitessier struck it about the head with the butt of his speargun, his assailant let go. Although it continued to prowl threateningly, it did not renew its attack and Moitessier was able to return to his boat.

RESCUERS UNHARMED

Shortly before Christmas 1958, Billy Weaver and several friends were surfing off a reef at Oahu, Hawaii. Weaver became isolated from the group when he missed a wave. When they heard him crying for help, they swam to him. He was alive, but they saw that he had lost a leg. At this point – some time after the original assault – the shark, a 7 metre (23ft) tiger, attacked again and the unfortunate Weaver disappeared. His body, missing most of the right leg, was later recovered.

On 8th May 1964 Sailasa Ratubalavu was spearfishing near a reef off Fiji. He had just caught a fish, still thrashing on his spear, when an unseen shark struck him violently from behind, tearing off his buttocks. As he screamed for help, a further strike removed his lower abdomen and genitalia. A fellow fisherman went to his aid. Remarkably, he was able to deter further attack, and eventually helped Ratubalavu back to their boat, but he died shortly after.

MYSTERY OF THE MISSING DIVER

One of the most macabre attacks on record occurred in July 1938 near Bathurst Island. A Japanese 'hard hat' diver named Okada had suffered an attack of the 'bends' and was being slowly raised to the surface. Suddenly the line from the boat went slack and was brought up with only Okada's corselet and helmet attached. It was presumed that he had been torn out of his equipment by a large shark.

DANGEROUS SHARKS IN PACIFIC WATERS

Great white shark
Mako shark (longfin and shortfin)
Tiger shark
Blue shark
Silvertip shark
Blacktip shark
Oceanic whitetip shark
Whitetip reef shark
Grey reef shark
Lemon shark
Galapagos shark
Hammerhead shark (great and scalloped)

Right: A native boy riding a nurse shark in the clear, shallow waters of Tahiti, appears unconcerned by the possible danger of his activity.

Attacks: New Zealand

ALTHOUGH quite a small country, the twin islands of New Zealand occupy a considerable range of latitude, from around 35 to 47 degrees south. The climate varies from cool temperate in the south to almost subtropical in the extreme north, with the surrounding seas consequently harbouring a diverse range of shark species.

Amongst the most dangerous shark species, the great white is widespread throughout New Zealand's waters, whilst the tiger shark's range surrounds practically the whole of North Island, at least in the warmer months. Other potentially dangerous species include the smooth hammerhead, bronze whaler, mako and blue shark.

The population of the country is small – less than 3.5 million – but most New Zealanders live within easy reach of the sea and water sports are highly popular. The coastal waters of New Zealand have been the setting for at least 30 confirmed shark attacks since the mid nineteenth century. Although this equates to a rate of little more than one attack every five years, it represents a threat many times higher per head of population than, for instance, Southern California. Of these attacks, ten are known to have been fatal, giving a survival rate consistent with other parts of the globe.

Overall, attacks appear to be distributed fairly randomly, with obvious concentrations around major centres of population. Most of these are easily explained by the prevalence of bathing and other water sports in the areas in question. However, the region around Dunedin in the far south would seem to support a cluster of seven attacks – out of proportion to the area's small population.

Five of the Dunedin attacks, of which no less than three were fatal, occurred in the years 1964 to 1971. Although in none of these instances was the species of shark reliably identified, the region's cool sub-Antarctic waters inevitably focus suspicion on the great white. It has even been suggested that a single individual was responsible for all the attacks, although this is pure speculation.

CHILLY, BUT FOR WHOM?

It was once believed that shark attacks were features of warm tropical oceans. Sir Victor Copplestone, the eminent Australian shark expert, proposed in 1933 that sea temperatures below 21°C (70°F) were not conducive to aggressive shark activity.

Even allowing for the fact that all but one of the Dunedin attacks took place in the warmer months, the waters in which they occurred fall well below that figure. It is more plausible that 21°C (70°F) is nearer the limit of comfort for human bathers rather than sharks. Most of the Dunedin five wore wetsuits, and all were engaged in specific physical activities: surfing, spearfishing or competitive swimming. The same phenomenon can be observed in other parts of the world, notably in that other great white 'stronghold' of northern California.

Left: A diver follows a baby tiger shark. This dangerous species is found in the oceans surrounding New Zealand's North Island, particularly in the warmer months.

Attacks: Africa

ALTHOUGH Africa as a whole ranks quite low in the shark attack league, this is probably due to the scarcity of reliable information rather than the actual incidence of cases. For South Africa, and in particular Natal, boasts one of the highest concentrations of confirmed attacks to be found anywhere on the globe.

In part, this is surely a reflection of the greater affluence of (white) South Africans: they are more likely to have leisure time to spend in the water. No less important must be the well established reporting methods present in this most advanced of all African countries.

The seas around South Africa itself can be divided into two main types. The Atlantic seaboard is washed by the north-flowing Benguela current. These cool waters support a different variety of shark species than are found in the warmer waters of the Indian Ocean. Indeed, the profile of species is similar to that of California. The chilly seas also deter bathing, and shark attacks are practically unknown.

The Natal coast of eastern South Africa is a different proposition entirely. The beaches around Durban, and further south at Amanzimtoti and Margate, have been notorious for shark attacks at least since the 1940s.

Amanzimtoti, a popular bathing area 32km (20 miles) south of Durban, is sometimes given the unhappy title of 'the worst shark attack beach on earth'. This one stretch of shore has over a dozen recorded attacks, including three in as many months in 1974. All occurred in murky water considered conducive to shark attack, with bathing prohibited at the time. Two of the victims were surfers, well offshore at

the moment they were struck. One had a leg amputated below the knee, one needed 19 stitches to a heel wound, whilst the third, James Gurr, had a miraculous escape.

Gurr's experience began ominously when he spotted a large shark heading directly for the surfboard he was riding.

The shark first knocked him from the board, then struck again as he was clambering back onto it, when he felt the shark against his chest. Despite one more violent strike, Gurr emerged from his adventure totally unscathed, although a clear imprint of his attacker's teeth was left on his surfboard.

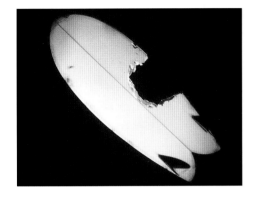

Above: This surfboard was attacked and bitten by a great white shark.

INLAND KILLERS

As to the rest of Africa, it is other countries bordering the Indian Ocean which report the highest rates of shark attack. Chief amongst these is Mozambique, where attacks have been recorded in both coastal and river water, the latter the work of the bull or Zambesi shark, *Carcharhinus luecas*. Although the bull does not grow to the immense sizes of killers such as the tiger or great white shark, its massive, heavily-muscled jaws and large teeth make it a formidable animal.

These notoriously aggressive creatures are known to range as much as 200km (125 miles) from open sea. For instance, three attacks occurred in a relatively small area near the mouth of the Limpopo River over a six month period early in 1961. All were attributed to the Zambesi shark. The same species was held responsible for a number of fatalities further north near Mogadishu, Somalia, during the seventies and eighties.

One of the more gruesome river attacks befell a fisherman in December 1970 in the Inhambane estuary, Mozambique. He was one of a group of men working on their prawn net, about 20km (12 miles) from open sea. He was standing neck-deep in the murky water when attacked by an unidentified shark, probably a bull shark. The first strike severed his arm at the shoulder. As he slipped below the water, the shark took off his head with a second strike, before his fellow fishermen drove it away.

Left: Tiger shark.   *Above: A popular beach, Natal, Durban.*

Above: Tiger sharks, like this one being man-handled, are common in African waters.

Like Australia, South Africa has been prominent with measures to safeguard bathing beaches. As long ago as 1907, a 200 metre (650ft) 'shark-proof' cage was installed near Durban. The steel structure remained effective until 1928 when serious corrosion set in. It was not replaced.

Surprisingly, shark nets were not introduced in Natal until the 1960s. This followed a series of seven attacks, five of them fatal, in the summer of 1967-8. The immediate response was one of wild panic, with bathers abandoning the beaches in droves and holiday trade plummeting. Before instituting proper shark control measures, the authorities even called in the navy to depth charge likely shark waters. The result of this misguided action was a bonanza of dead fish which only served to attract more sharks to the area. Netting was later introduced, based largely on practices found effective in New South Wales. This has substantially reduced the incidence of shark attacks, although they have not been completely eliminated.

South Africa has also been at the forefront of medical response to shark attack, for which Barbara Strauss had reason to be thankful when attacked off the north Natal coast in December 1963. Miss Strauss was standing with two friends in waist-deep water when a 1.8 metre (6ft) grey shark repeatedly struck her, having brushed against her companions in the process. Her wounds were grave, with the right hand and foot severed and the right buttock almost denuded of flesh.

Fortunately the victim received prompt treatment, along guidelines laid down by the Oceanographic Research Institute of Durban. Before being moved to hospital, Miss Strauss' condition was stabilised by stopping bleeding, administering a plasma transfusion, placing her in a head-down position and keeping her warm. Despite her horrific injuries, she survived.

Above: An oceanic whitetip shark.

Attacks: Europe

TO MOST of us the Mediterranean is a benign blue sea, less an ocean than a watery playground. Certainly most holidaymakers are oblivious to the threat that lurks beneath its tideless waters, and it would be surprising if the tourist industry sought to make them better informed. Most of the 45 species of shark found in the Mediterranean are harmless to man. But at least one is not. For the great white shark is widespread from Port Said to Gibraltar.

It would be surprising if it were otherwise. The earliest accounts of great white attacks (see p45) are from the Mediterranean. Earlier still, a three million year old dolphin fossil shows characteristic marks consistent with great white attack. Great whites were visiting Mediterranean waters long before the first human holidaymakers traipsed south to the beaches.

Above: Accounts of attacks by great white sharks in the Mediterranean date back to the Greek historian Herodotus (485-425BC).
Below: European fishermen often encounter sharks around their nets.

There is certainly no doubt that very large sharks live in this sea. A specimen landed at Malta in 1987 measured over 7.1 metres (23ft 3in) in length. Sicilian tuna fisherman frequently report great whites in or around their nets during the annual kill. They also have a saying – 'if you see a female, the male will not be far behind' – which suggests a doubling of menace.

Yet considering the huge numbers of holidaymakers attracted to Mediterranean beaches, the risk is almost infinitesimally small. Since 1909 perhaps 40 people have been attacked by sharks, of whom 18 died. Most, if not all of these, are thought to be the work of the great white – *Carcharodon carcharias*.

Attacks have been reported off the coasts of Italy, Greece, Egypt, Malta, Tunisia, Israel, France and the former Yugoslavia. The 'hot spot' appears to be a triangular region roughly bordered by Sicily, Malta and North Africa, which is also thought to be an important breeding ground for great whites. The western Mediterranean appears comparatively safe.

The pattern of attacks is much as elsewhere. Danger is heightened at night, in murky water, and in the presence of sea-borne debris. It is often associated with floating objects such as canoes or surfboards, which are thought to arouse the shark's curiosity.

The Mediterranean also hosted the only recorded attack of a great white on a wind surfer, off the coast of Terife, Spain. The shark first struck the board, then struck again, severing the man's foot.

In a widely-reported attack in 1989, a scuba diver, Luciano Constanzo, was attacked whilst removing fouling from an underwater cable in the Gulf of Baratti. Practically all of his equipment was recovered – including his webbing belts, still fastened – but no trace of the diver himself was found.

The common phenomenon of attacks on inanimate objects was illustrated again in July 1978 when a shark attacked a large oceanographic research platform with sufficient vigour to disturb its occupants. The culprit? 'Squalo bianco' – the great white.

Some authorities have suggested that 'Mediterranean' great whites were no more than occasional visitors from the Atlantic. They pointed to the decimation of what was thought to be their principal food – seals – as evidence that the sea could not sustain a significant great white population.

More recent research, however, points to a favoured diet of tuna and dolphin. Yet this also carries a threat to the great white far more potent than the tiny risk it bears to man. Overfishing and pollution impose a heavy toll on all marine life. Tuna catches are but a fraction of the abundance of four decades ago – a problem as much for the shark as for Latin fishermen. The Adriatic, where the great white was common at one time, is now one of the most degraded seas on earth. The great white's days in the Mediterranean may very well be numbered.

Below: Great whites often come to the surface, to investigate floating objects.

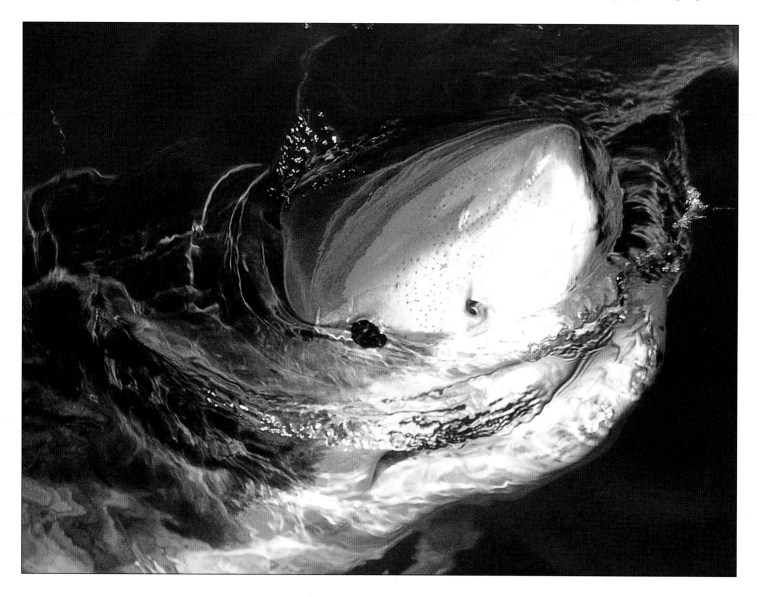

Attacks: Great Britain

YOU ARE probably more likely to be struck twice by lightning than attacked by a shark in British waters. Indeed, the latter is the more desirable option, as none of the few recorded attacks have been fatal.

The most northerly shark attack in British, or any other, waters took place off Wick, Scotland on 27 June 1960 when a fisherman, Hans Joachim Schaper, was bitten on the arm by a small shark. Most other attacks in British waters can be viewed as similar 'incidental', almost predictable hazards of fishing, rather than nightmarish unprovoked strikes.

Other recorded attacks in British waters are rare. In 1937, two sailing boats were attacked, possibly by the same shark, also in Scottish waters. And in August 1960, one William Chapel was injured by an unidentified species of shark off Devon. Again, this was not an 'unprovoked' attack. Chapel was in the process of landing a 36kg (79lbs) shark hooked by an angler.

No doubt there are many other instances of fishermen injured whilst landing sharks, but these are presumably too minor – or too embarrassing – to warrant formal notification.

Sharks are not commonplace off British beaches, although during the summer months they are found in quite large numbers in our offshore waters. Several West Country holiday resorts host buoyant recreational shark fisheries. Threshers and porbeagles also regularly come up-Channel during the annual mackerel run, when they are particularly common off the rocky headlands of the Isle of Wight.

On 1 June 1971, Jimmy Johnson, a 32-year old scuba diver, was attacked within 50 metres (170ft) of the beach off Beesands, Devon. He drove off repeated attacks by what was believed to be a 3.6 metre (12ft) mako (possibly a porbeagle) with a lobster hook, before returning to shore unharmed.

But sharks are better known in British waters for the pleasure they give: either the bloodthirsty thrill of hooking a porbeagle off the Cornish coast, or the magnificent sight of a giant basking shark cruising the green waters off Scotland or the Isle of Man.

Left: Scottish fishermen are more likely to see a basking shark than a man-eater.

JOHN O'GROATS JOURNAL, FRIDAY 8 JULY 1960:

An 18 year-old German seaman was taken to the Bignold Hospital, Wick, on Wednesday for treatment to a shark bite.

Hans Joachim Schaper was a crew member of the trawler *I Mai*. The incident occurred ten days earlier. Schaper was bitten on the right arm by a small shark which was discovered entangled in the net after it was hauled on deck.

The wound became septic and he was transferred to another East German trawler, the *Karl Marx*, which landed him at Wick harbour after midnight on Tuesday.

Herr Schaper was able to return to his ship later.

Attacks: Rest of the World

NUMERICALLY, the seas safest from shark attack are the Arctic and Antarctic oceans, a chilly statistic which offers little comfort to the casual bather. Whilst such waters undoubtedly support sharks capable of attacking humans, for obvious reasons their opportunity to do so is almost non-existent. The most northerly attack on record (see page 63) was at a latitude of only 58 degrees.

Although shark attacks have been recorded in all other temperate and tropical oceanic waters, their frequency in many huge tracts of the globe is ostensibly rare. South America, for instance, contributes around one half of one per cent of all known attacks. Yet even this is half as much again as all the attacks recorded for all the islands of the Indian Ocean.

Above: In less developed countries of the world, there are probably many shark attack victims who remain unrecorded by the compilers of statistical data.

Right: Photographed in the Caribbean Sea, this diver has provoked a small shark into arching its back in an aggressive posture – a warning signal that it may attack.

SOUTH & CENTRAL AMERICA

Although reports of shark attack throughout this huge region are rare, the great white again features as a principal offender. Even the navy is at risk.

In August 1943 a US Navy motor torpedo boat put to in a cove off Ray Island in the Gulf of Panama to investigate vibration in its drive system. After the MTB had been stationary in the water for some time, a sailor dived overboard to check the propeller. He was immediately subjected to a furious attack from a 2 metre (6¹/₂ft) shark. Although quickly hauled back on board, the victim died from shock and blood loss some hours later, mainly due to massive leg and shoulder wounds. Teeth fragments showed the shark to have been a great white, perhaps surprising in view of the tropical location.

Alfredo Aubone's horrifying encounter with a great white ended less tragically. In January 1954 Aubone was floating in 5 metres (16¹/₂ft) of water about 100 metres (325ft) from shore near Mar de Plate, Argentina. There were several other bathers nearby, the closest within 1 metre (3¹/₂ft). Suddenly Aubone felt his arm grabbed, followed by at least another two violent strikes. Then, despite much blood in the water, the shark – identified as a great white from tooth fragments – appeared to lose interest and swam off. Aubone recovered from his injuries.

Although pre-emptive aggressive behaviour towards sharks is normally ill-advised, once an attack has begun this may be the only means of escape. In 1956 Gabriel Echavarria was spearfishing with his father and another companion off the coast of the Isles of Rosario, near Cartagena, Columbia. Whilst young Gabriel was busy with a speared fish, his father noticed a nearby (unidentified) shark behaving oddly. He continued to watch as the shark slowly approached his son and struck at his foot. As the shark appeared to be ready for a second strike, the father speared it and it swam off. Although the victim was quite badly wounded, his diving flipper saved him from more serious injury.

Of the areas of the world not dealt with in specific chapters, the shores of the Indian Ocean and Central America appear to be the hot-spots for attacks. According to the Shark Attack File, India, Iran and Aden between them account for nearly three per cent of recorded attacks, with the Red Sea and Persian Gulf adding almost another one per cent.

Central America contributes over 1.5 per cent of the known total, of which the vast majority have occurred along the Caribbean or Pacific coasts of Panama.

It is almost certain that all these figures are gross under-estimates, caused partly by reporting methods which are primitive (if they exist at all), partly by local cultures which perhaps regard shark attack as but one more hazard in an intrinsically hazardous way of life. Some estimates – or guesses – put the annual number of shark attacks world wide as high as 1000, of which perhaps three quarters take place off the shores of Africa, Asia and South America. If so, this makes the 'official' figures pale into insignificance.

There is some evidence that as countries develop, the incidence of attacks rises. It is probably no coincidence that of all the countries mentioned above, the one with by far the highest rate of shark attack for its size is Panama, a strategically important site with a relatively well developed bureaucracy and tourist industry. As in war, it seems, as many victims probably go unknown and unsung as find their way into official records.

None of this detracts from the tragedy of individual shark attacks, nor from the acts of courage which often accompany them. The bravery displayed in the following attack, in Telegraph Bay, Aden, has perhaps been repeated a thousand times by unsung heroes elsewhere. In September 1955, when a female bather was attacked by a 2.3 metre (7ft) shark, Mohammed Arecki went to her rescue. Armed with an iron bar, he was able to beat off repeated attacks, both on himself and the original victim, whom he eventually managed to bring onto the shore. The woman later died of her injuries, which included the severance of part of an arm and a leg.

Mass Attacks

ALTHOUGH it is difficult to countenance the horror of even a single, isolated shark attack, falling victim to a mass feeding frenzy of sharks far out in open water must be one of the most terrifying experiences. The death rates from such incidents are inevitably high, as help is rarely near at hand and victims are often already weak from injury or lack of food and water. The Greek historian Herodotus reported the first such disaster when sharks set upon Persian sailors almost 2500 years ago, but there have been many since.

In October 1926 the British patrol boat *Valerian* sank in shark-infested waters 28km (17 miles) south west of Bermuda. Of the crew of 104, a mere 20 survived repeated attacks by sharks.

Native canoeists travelling between the Ellice Islands were attacked by large numbers of sharks at night. A feeding frenzy developed, from which only two of an estimated 40 islanders survived.

In 1934 a Chinese junk sank instantly after a collision with a British destroyer.

Accounts speak of a frenzied pack of sharks converging on the scene and attacking the junk's 11 man crew. Only one survived.

On 28 November 1942 the troopship *Nova Scotia* sank after taking a torpedo hit from a German submarine, 50km (31 miles) from the South African coast. It is believed that most of the 900 men on board (including 756 Italian prisoners of war) survived the sinking. However, during the next 2½ days the survivors suffered repeated shark

Left: An engraving dated 1904, showing sharks attacking four young girls.
Above: The jaws of death.

attacks as they lay in the water. A mere 192 men were rescued. Many of their dead colleagues were still floating from their life jackets with much of their lower bodies missing.

When another troopship, the *Cape San Juan*, was torpedoed in the South Pacific on 11 November one year later, a great deal worse than drowning awaited many of the allied troops on board. Just 448 of the 1429 aboard were subsequently rescued by the mer-

chant ship *Edwin T Merridith*. Even when rescue operations were in progress, frenzied sharks were reported to be hurling themselves onto life rafts to snatch survivors.

Possibly the most notorious World War II shark disaster, which was later made into a movie starring Stacy Keach, concerned the American cruiser *SS Indianapolis*. Whilst returning from Tinian Island where it had delivered several vital components for the Hiroshima atom bomb, the *Indianapolis* was torpedoed by the Japanese submarine *I.58* on 30 July 1945.

Many of the cruiser's crew of

almost 1200 made it safely into the water, where they remained for four days before assistance arrived. During this time a large number (estimates vary from 50 to 100) were taken by sharks, and many of the survivors suffered non-fatal bites as the bloody waters encouraged successive waves of strikes. In total 883 seamen lost their lives, the worst disaster at sea in US naval history.

In March 1975 a ferry capsized in the Ganges-Brahmaputra delta of Bangladesh, casting an estimated 190 passengers and crew into the water. It is believed that as many as 50 of the casualties succumbed to shark attack.

Provoked Attacks

IT IS important to distinguish between the unprovoked shark attacks that are numerically the most common, and attacks in which the victim (or his companions) play some part in encouraging an assault. This is particularly true of fishermen, divers and spearfishermen who are at the highest risk, by far, of shark attack. The first such attack was recorded as long ago as 1892, when a diver named Rotoman was bitten literally in two by a shark he had deliberately provoked with a knife.

Surface fishermen, whether landing sharks by accident or design, often suffer injuries. Any animal which feels threatened will attempt to defend itself, usually either by fighting back, or by fleeing. Whilst sharks will opt for the quieter approach surprisingly often in open water, being hauled onto the deck of a boat obviously denies them this possibility.

The risk is made worse by the difficulty of killing a shark. In common with eels, this primitive animal seems almost impervious to any amount of clubbing and wounding. However, unlike the eel, most sharks are handsomely armed. Reports often speak of sharks 'coming back from the dead' to wreak havoc in the confined space of a fishing boat. Even species generally regarded as harmless in their usual environment have inflicted quite serious injuries, with limbs sometimes lost. It is little wonder that two of the very few incidents of shark attack known in UK waters were to fishermen.

Divers, too, run a heightened risk of shark attack. This is especially true if they become over-confident or playful, for sharks have little sense of fun. Even 'harmless' filter-feeders such as the basking or whale shark can inflict painful, if accidental, injury with a lash of their coarse-skinned tail. Passive species such as the nurse shark (*Ginglymostoma cirratum*) have also been aroused into biting over-enthusiastic divers.

Spearfishing is perhaps the most risky of all 'provocative' activities. A struggling, wounded fish – the point of the exercise, after all – is practically a beacon to any prowling shark, drawing it to the scene and arousing feeding behaviour. In known shark waters it can be likened to carrying a butchered animal through a lion park – not exactly prudent behaviour.

But perhaps most at risk of all is the spearfisherman who attempts to spear a shark. Sharks show an understandable pique at being prodded, let alone shot, with something sharp, and often strike back at their persecutors. An injured shark can be a terrifying proposition.

FLYING FISH

Even when seeking other species, fishermen can be at risk. On 19th June 1935 Captain Manuel Chalor was about to land a large bluefish off the New Jersey coast when to his alarm a 5 metre (16½ft) shark flew past him, landing on the deck of his small craft. In the ensuing panic, Chalor slipped and found his arm in the shark's jaws. The rest of the crew eventually encouraged the creature to let go by pelting it with a hail of wood and hardware. Only when struck on the head with an old harpoon did it finally slip back into the sea. Chalor made a full recovery.

Left: Divers often become over-confident with sharks, and take unnecessary risks with them, forgetting that sharks are not playful, fun-loving creatures.

Above: When provoked, sharks will often display this aggressive, 'hump-backed' posture. This signal should not be ignored, as an attack may follow.

CAMERA SHY

One man who took provocation to extremes was stuntman Frank Donahue. Prior to filming a sequence requiring him to wrestle a 2 metre (6½ft) shark, Donahue went searching for a suitable specimen off Santa Monica, California. When he finally found a shark of the prescribed size, he grabbed its tail and hauled it aboard his boat. All might have gone to script had he not slipped, allowing his reluctant co-star to bite deep into his arm.

ASKING FOR TROUBLE

One man who learned his lesson the hard way was Troy Dicks, a South African. On 30th May 1959 Dicks and a companion were spearfishing near Port Elizabeth when they noticed a great white shark. They swam towards the creature, which in turn approached them. Dicks then shot it with his speargun, whereupon the shark, not surprisingly, turned on him. Dicks wrestled with the shark and was able to blast it with compressed gas by triggering his un-armed speargun into its jaws. This may have earned him the precious seconds of respite during which his companion was able to fatally wound the fish with a spear to the gills. Dicks later vowed never to shoot a shark again.

SPEARED!

Even quite small sharks can be dangerous when provoked, as Andres Pruna discovered in May 1967 near Key West, Florida. Pruna had just speared a 0.9 metre (3ft) nurse shark, minding its own business under a ledge. The shark was recovered from the spear and hit on the head until dead – or so it seemed. The shark suddenly sprang to life, biting Pruna on the ankle. With some difficulty he shook it free, and the shark swam off.

Even experienced native fishermen can make similar mistakes. In September 1970 Palau Islander Aisameral Samsel was spearfishing off the reef when one of his four companions shot a 0.9 metre (3ft) shark. The fish responded by turning on Samsel, inflicting quite serious injuries to his left forearm.

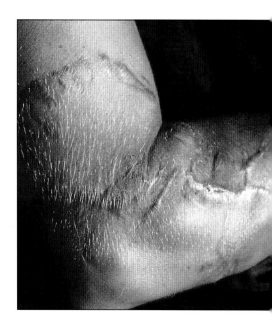

Above: This scarred arm is the result of a great white shark attack.
Left: Any great white shark is a dangerous creature and a large one, like this, is potentially lethal.

COMIC CUTS

Some attacks, if only in retrospect, are almost comic. In April 1949 a US warship was demonstrating its guns and depth charges to the Mexican military off Tampico. Suddenly a shark, supposedly terrified by the racket, threw itself onto Miramar beach and bit a bather. Other bathers quickly beat the fish to death.

A tale of just deserts took place off Quinby, Virginia in July 1970 when a sports fisherman thrust a troop-training firecracker into a small shark's mouth and threw it back overboard. The fish swam under the 10 metre (33ft) boat, the firecracker exploded, the hull split and the vessel sank.

Victims

DURING this century there have been, on average, around 30 reported cases of shark attack per year, of which roughly one-third are fatal. In recent decades the survival rate has fallen steadily to well below that figure, perhaps through the intervention of improved medical care.

Most victims are recreational swimmers, for no better reason than that is the activity that takes most people into the sea. For similar reasons, around nine tenths of all attacks take place within 1.6 metres (5ft) of the surface, usually in shallow water. However, as a group, divers are statistically most at risk. The deepest-ever known attack took place at a depth of some 90 metres (300ft).

In around two thirds of all attacks the victim was in water waist deep or less. In a similar proportion, the shark was unseen until the instant of attack.

Most victims are male. Again, this is probably to be expected, since males tend to go into the sea more often and for longer, and are more likely to be scuba divers. Nonetheless there is something about the proportions that begs the question as to whether there is something about females – their behaviour, perhaps, or even some olfactory characteristic – which renders them less susceptible.

Sharks are almost certainly indifferent to race, but there is some evidence to suggest that uneven tanning offers a high contrast target on which sharks can more readily home in. The able-bodied appear as much at risk as weak or injured bathers. Although it would

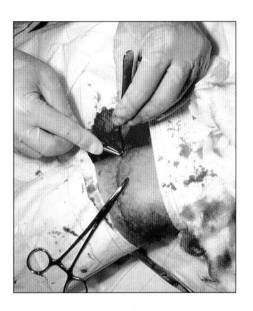

Above: This diver receives surgery to repair a fairly minor shark bite.
Below left: Diver Henri Bource lost his leg to a great white of about this size.

probably be wise not to take a fresh wound into known shark waters, there is no direct evidence that this encourages aggressive shark behaviour. The same is true of menstruation.

Of all the individual 'types' of sea users, divers are the group most at risk, and far more likely to be attacked than people swimming off a beach. Yet, perhaps because they are more at home underwater and are more likely to see their assailant, their injuries are usually far less severe than those of surface swimmers. One thing that appears to tip the balance the other way, however, is spearfishing, which drastically raises the potential for shark attack.

Surface fishermen, too, can put themselves at risk. Even a small shark can be dangerous when landed. Unless already badly wounded, sharks take a great deal of time to die once removed from the water – often over 30 minutes.

NATURE OF ATTACK

Many attacks are preceded by an exploratory nudge or bump. These do not always lead to a full-blooded strike. Indeed it may be that, on occasions when they do not, the victim did not even suspect that a shark was responsible.

Often, however, such initial bumps are of sufficient violence to leave no-one in any doubt that something terrible is afoot. Many accounts speak of victims being thrown bodily out of the water by the sheer force of the charge.

Where a victim is in a position to see the attacker, the assault is just as likely to arrive head-on as from the side or rear. Sharks, it seems, are not disposed to sneak up on their victims.

However terrifying they might be, there is some reason for believing that many – perhaps most – shark attacks are not motivated by hunger. The typical shark attack comprises one or two strikes, whilst only a quarter are pursued to an extent that suggests an overriding feeding impulse. In only perhaps 15 per cent of cases does it seem that the shark is intent on finishing off his victim.

FRENZIED ATTACKS

Anybody unfortunate enough to find themselves in the midst of a number of frenzied sharks has very little chance of survival. Three youths were surprised by a wave whilst swimming off Rio Haina in the Dominican Republic in 1963. One of them managed to clamber ashore, but the other two were set upon by a group estimated at eight sharks. One, according to an eye-witness account, 'was thrown into the air like a basket-ball, and while in the air another shark took a bite out of his belly'. Within seconds, the victims were gone. Thankfully multiple shark attacks are rare, perhaps less than six per cent of all cases, whilst frenzied attacks by individual sharks are rarer still.

Below: This shark has been attracted to the camera by the smell and taste of fresh blood. It is wise not to take a fresh wound into known shark waters.

INJURIES

Even a sharp swipe from a shark's rough hide or a fin can cause grave injury. However, by far the most common are obviously biting injuries, which almost invariably cause considerable tissue loss with large chunks of flesh being removed down to the bone. Limbs, or parts of limbs, are frequently lost.

Leg injuries are the most common result of shallow water attacks, themselves the most common form of attack. Most victims survive the immediate attack. Fatalities arise from shock and rapid blood loss, typically within minutes if the main artery of the leg, the femoral artery, is severed.

Traumatic shock can rapidly lead to death even in those victims still conscious and coherent when returned to the safety of boat or shore. Experience suggests that the best practice is not immediate transfer to hospital, but sound paramedic measures to stabilise the patient, much in the manner of road traffic casualties. For some years major South African beaches have been equipped with emergency packs containing morphine, saline and plasma, for precisely this purpose. Rushing badly injured victims to hospital by car can sometimes be the worst possible remedy.

In the days before antibiotics, victims who survived blood loss and shock frequently succumbed to infections, often in a disturbingly brief time. Septicemia and gangrene were major killers before the advent of penicillin. Deep, incised wounds are most susceptible. Nonetheless, a 30 year old female attacked near Sydney in 1924 had one leg severed and the other foot lacerated to the bone, yet managed to haul herself ashore in great pain. She recovered full health and was discharged from hospital 1½ months later.

Right: This dummy diver is being used to assess the way sharks attack humans.

RESCUERS

It must be an act of supreme bravery to intervene in any but the most minor shark attack. And yet, would-be rescuers and bystanders fare surprisingly well during shark attacks, although this can be little consolation to most victims. It seems as though the assailant, once he has targeted a victim, is unwilling or unable to change his target. The only exception appears to be in the confusion of genuinely frenzied attacks, particularly where several sharks are concerned. And, of course, in the sort of mass shark attacks which sometimes occur after shipwrecks.

In September 1931 a hammerhead shark attacked a woman off Palm Beach, Florida. Although the shark continued to follow the victim's blood trail, the life-guard who came to her aid was able to make it draw back by aggressively beating the water. The woman survived, despite serious leg injuries.

Wounds received by rescuers are usually minor, chiefly grazing injuries caused by the attacker's coarse skin. For instance, when a 5 metre (16½ft) shark attacked a spearfisherman in 2 metres (6½ft) of water in the Solomon Islands in September 1963, it had to swim past his companion to do so. The companion then went to the victim's aid, dragging him at least 200 metres (650 ft) to shore. The shark followed for most of this distance, but did not renew the attack.

REMAINS – THE SHARK GIVES UP ITS SECRET

In most instances of shark attack it is the victim, his companions, or onlookers who report the incident. Many cases of fatal attacks involving lone individuals must go unreported. But perhaps the most gruesome of all reporting 'methods' is the recovery of human remains from sharks captured or found washed ashore.

The digestive process of most sharks is quite slow, meaning that

Above: A diver receives prompt medical attention after a minor shark bite.
Left: Great whites are not fussy eaters.

stomach contents may remain identifiably human for several days.

Perhaps the best-known illustration of shark's leisurely digestion was noted in April 1935. A 4.3 metre (14ft) tiger shark had been captured unharmed and placed in the Coogee Aquarium in the coastal suburbs of Sydney. Fully eight days later the shark regurgitated a human arm, bound at the wrist and bearing a tattoo that led to the identification of its former owner. As a macabre post-script, it was surmised that this was the aftermath of an attempt to dispose of the body of a murder victim. A man was later charged with this and other crimes but not convicted.

A more conventional instance came to light in July 1953 when the decomposing body of a 2.7 metre (9ft) shark was found in Galveston Bay, Texas. It may not have warranted further investigation, except that what appeared to be a human foot protruded from its side. When the stomach was opened, it revealed most of the body of a youth, with only the head, shoulders and arms missing. The body was never identified.

In March 1944 a fisherman off Venice, Florida caught a large tiger shark. Inside, he found an unknown man's body, from the lower ribs to the knees. Ten years later in October 1954 the stomach of a one tonne/ton shark caught near Nagasaki held the body of a teenage boy, still clad in shirt and trousers. Again, the unfortunate victim was never identified.

In some cases, however, the poor victim is known long before the shark gives up its meal. One widely reported case as long ago as 8th November 1911 took place in Pensacola Bay, Florida, before some 50 onlookers (at least one of whom fainted). As they looked on, a shark suddenly appeared at the surface, bearing a man in its jaws. This, it transpired, was Jules Antoine, a ship's watchman, who had somehow ended up in the water. The shark dived, then surfaced again, but now grasping only the head of its victim. When the 3.6 metre (12ft) shark was killed the next day by a posse raised by the affronted citizens, it was found to contain almost the whole of Antoine's body.

One slightly suspect report describes the death of a Cuban man who fell into the sea and was immediately set upon by a shark which bit off his leg. The man's friend promptly dived into the water, killed the shark and recovered the victim's leg so that he could be buried 'whole'.

If this latter case carries with it a sense of old-world nobility, this is not always the case. Perhaps the greater loss is that even in so-called 'advanced' countries with their shifting populations, many of the remains recovered from sharks are never identified. To be eaten by a shark is an horrific end for any person, but to go unmissed surely adds indignity to tragedy.

Counter Measures

THERE IS only one absolutely sure way of avoiding shark attack: don't go near the water. But such advice is ridiculous in the extreme. Most people are not deterred, quite rightly, by the tiny number of shark attacks which occur each year. Yet they – and the holiday communities which depend on their patronage – would be wise to take basic counter measures.

'Anti-shark' measures are many and varied. Some involve special equipment, and some do not. The most basic 'rule' in shark areas would be to avoid bathing in murky waters, particularly at night or when there is floating debris about, and obviously to heed any posted warnings.

As to more active measures, banging or shouting has been alleged to frighten sharks away. Yet the same techniques have been employed by shark photographers to attract sharks nearer to the camera. It seems as likely that they will provoke as deter an approach from an inquisitive shark.

Anyone unfortunate enough to find himself floating in known shark waters is best advised to stay calm; conserve energy; do not remove clothing (to preserve heat as well as offering some protection from a brush with the coarse skin of a curious shark); and to huddle together with companions. Such groups not only appear to reduce the risk of attack, but help conserve heat. It should

be remembered that exposure and exhaustion are usually far greater threats in such situations than are sharks.

CHEMICAL REPELLENTS
Of the specialized anti-shark measures, perhaps the best-known are chemical repellents. The first of these, 'Shark Chaser' was developed by the US Navy during World War II. It relied on the fishermen's 'fact' (since much disputed) that sharks avoid the dead of their own kind, and included copper acetate

Below: Testing repellent on a blue shark.
Right: Many of the world's most notorious shark beaches are protected by strong nets to shield bathers from attack.

which was believed to mimic the offending chemical. A dye was also incorporated to add a visual screen to the chemical one. The British Navy produced a similar repellent, imaginatively titled 'Admiralty Pattern 0473/1399'.

Early tests suggested that *Shark Chaser* was effective in repelling sharks, and possession of the 10 x 7 x 2cm (4 x 3 x 3/4in) packs was certainly a morale-booster for sailors. The sharks were rather less impressed, even being observed eating packs of *Shark Chaser*. Later tests confirmed that the compound had no effect on sharks whatsoever. With the end of the war the need for such a repellent all-but disappeared, and the search for an effective repellent practically ceased.

There is still no proven shark repellent, although several interesting avenues are being pursued. Recent research has focused on naturally occurring repellent compounds, for it would be surprising if at least one ocean-

dweller had not found an effective chemical survival aid in an environment dominated by sharks. Many land creatures, after all, are so equipped. The best-known of these is holothurian, found in sea cucumbers – a species rarely troubled by sharks, but quickly rejected if taken by mistake.

Another naturally occurring compound is a milky substance secreted by special glands on a small group of flatfish, *Pardachirus*, of which the best-known is the Moses sole. Very small quantities of this substance have been shown to repel sharks for as long as 18 hours. However, the complex chemical responsible has proved extremely difficult to synthesize and troublesome to store. However, other studies suggest that certain forms of industrial detergents may have similar effects. For a while an anaesthetic known as 'MS-222' also looked promising. This successfully immobilizes fish, but has little or no effect on sharks.

SHARK NETS

If a practical chemical barrier cannot be found, then why not a physical one? Many of the world's most notorious shark beaches, notably in South Africa and Australia, are now protected by nets. Such a system is inevitably expensive, both to install and maintain, and an economically viable proposition only in richer countries and for relatively small areas of shoreline. However, it does work. The shark cage is the diver's mobile equivalent of the shark net.

Another form of 'net' is the bubble curtain, developed in Australia in the early 1960s. Compressed air was pumped through a perforated hose laid on the sea bed, and the resulting wall of bubbles was held to form a barrier through which sharks would not pass. Sadly the originators of the idea appear not to have done their homework. Later tests in the Bahamas showed that, of twelve tiger sharks, eleven swam through the curtain with impunity.

MESHING

In some areas, nets are also used to reduce the possibility of attack by catching sharks, rather than simply keeping them out to sea. Known as 'meshing', this method relies on pairs of usually parallel nets, each around 150 metres (500ft) long and perhaps 500 metres (1650ft) from shore. Sharks attempting to find a way through the nets are trapped by their gills and suffocate, and are removed every couple of days by special maintenance teams. Like barrier nets, such a system is expensive, as well as indiscriminately catching a great deal of 'innocent' marine life.

ELECTRICAL

In South Africa a great deal of research has attempted to exploit the shark's acute sensitivity to electric fields. Sharks confronted by a small electric current above a certain threshold level will 'startle' and swim away rapidly. If the voltage is increased to another critical level, sharks display an 'electrotaxic' reaction in swimming towards the positive electrode. A higher voltage still can cause paralysis and death through suffocation – 'electronarcosis'.

Although an electrical barrier system based on these findings may have some potential for safer beaches, and a working prototype has been successfully tested, the cost of such an installation is, so far, prohibitive.

Several versions of personal electro-repellent have been developed. One of these, *Shark Shield*, has enjoyed success in protecting fishing nets from assaults by shark, but is considered too impractical and unwieldy by divers. A hand-held 'electric harpoon' has also been developed, but this again has proved too expensive to be viable.

Right: Many divers would welcome a shark repellent that is guaranteed to work. Here, a lemon shark attacks a flipper.

ARMOUR

If the beach isn't netted, why not net the bather? This is the rationale behind the *Neptunic*, basically a modern, stainless steel version of chain-mail. The *Neptunic* has proved effective in minimising the effect of shark bites but, at around £5000 per suit, its use is unlikely to become widespread. The same is true of suits made of space-age materials such as *Kevlar*, which offer similar anti-shark benefits.

Another form of personal shark barrier is the deceptively simple *Shark Screen*. This is intended for air and shipwreck victims rather than divers, and comprises a large plastic bag supported by inflatable rings, inside which the user floats. These have proved very effective against shark attack, as well as providing a useful measure of general survival protection. They can even be used as bivouac tents on land.

OFFENSIVE WEAPONS

Several aggressive devices have been developed, mainly for use by scuba divers who are the group far most at risk from shark attack. The earliest of these, developed by Jacques Cousteau, was simply a long pole topped by a small crown of nails. The nails were intended not to harm the fish, but to prevent the stick slipping off its tough hide. The 'shark billy' was intended merely to ward off a curious shark rather than do it harm, and was effective in experienced hands. An electrified version of the simple billy, the *Shark Tazer*, has also been produced.

As to more hostile measures, knives and even spearguns have little effect, such is the toughness of a shark's skin and constitution. Indeed, they may serve to turn what was merely curiosity into a full-blooded attack.

Because of this, several far more damaging weapons have been developed. The 'bang stick' is a pole tipped with a modified shotgun cartridge which explodes on contact with a shark. The 'powerhead' is a similarly-equipped speargun. Both are capable of mortally wounding even a large shark, but present a comparable danger to the diver and his companions – not least through accidental discharges on shore.

CO_2 darts comprise a small gas cylinder attached to a robust hollow needle. Again, this discharges on contact with a shark's hide, injecting a large bubble of gas into its body cavity. This makes the fish buoyant, forcing it to the surface, usually with fatal consequences. It requires extreme skill to use the dart, which is only effective from below and from the sides.

For the typical holidaymaker, the threat from sharks is slight enough to be ignored. What should be remembered is that other risks might be present, and that it is always worth taking local advice and heeding local warnings. Stepping barefoot on a sea urchin is enough to ruin most people's vacation. And never forget that the sea itself is the biggest killer: enjoy it, but treat it with respect.

Below: Looking like an underwater knight in armour, this diver is wearing a stainless steel shark suit as protection against attack.
Right: Taking photographs of sharks is a dangerous activity, not for the nervous!

Living with Sharks

WHATEVER else it might be, for many people the shark is an object of fascination at least as potent as the supposedly hypnotic qualities of the swaying cobra. Undoubtedly, part of this fascination arises from the sheer grace of a shark in motion. To those aware of it, the physical and sensory sophistication of this predatory fish must also play a part.

But so, too, does danger. Just as people climb mountains, race fast cars, bungee jump from cliffs and free-fall from aeroplanes, so other people seek a 'buzz' from close encounters with sharks.

Sometimes the justification for such risks is research, either purely scientific studies or for the filming of documentary programmes. The French naturalist Jacques-Yves Cousteau is perhaps the individual best known for combining both. But more often the motivation is the sheer joy of witnessing sharks in their natural habitat.

Yet even for serious observers, the shark is clearly an object of wonder. In describing 'the splendid savage of the sea', Cousteau wrote of the shark's 'nonchalant suspicion', of the 'murderous yet beautiful force' of his 'miraculous' presence. In Cousteau's time, much less was known about shark behaviour than is understood today, and the pioneering activities of the *Calypso's* crew were as brave as they were enlightening.

DIVING WITH SHARKS

Despite their fearsome reputation, most sharks are timid creatures which will avoid man rather than confront him. For the most part this is true even of individuals from species which are known man-eaters.

Swimming with the giant 'harmless' sharks – filter feeders like the basking and whale shark – is a rare and priceless treat for experienced divers. The basking shark is relatively common even in British waters, although our murky water conditions usually preclude close encounters with it. The chief danger in such situations is abrasion from the fish's rough hide, or of being struck accidentally by its powerful tail.

In several regions of the tropical oceans, notably the Maldives, parts of the Caribbean and Australia, underwater shark watching has become a popular recreational activity. Local shark specialists take groups of scuba divers on shark 'safaris'. In some localities, even potentially dangerous species of

Below: Sharks are usually more timid than this and avoid contact with divers.

shark have become so accustomed to these intrusions that they can be fed – cautiously – by hand. In others, divers may have the chance to stroke normally docile species such as the nurse shark.

But what of more aggressive species? Remarkably, many experienced shark watchers can describe occasions when they have encountered killers such as large tiger sharks without suffering harm or even threat. More often than not the 'man-eater' has seemed indifferent, even aloof, or merely mildly curious. Left to its own devices, it seems, a shark is far less hostile than most large land carnivores.

But, needless to say, no-one should embark on such activities without expert guidance from someone familiar with local sharks and their behaviour. Every shark expert has had cause to comment on the capacity of individuals or entire schools to change mood for no clear reason, and it is essential to be alert for such signs.

SHARK CAGES

The safest underwater vantage point of all would appear to be the so-called 'shark-proof' cage, a structure of (usually) aluminium tubes suspended from the stern of a boat. Cages are often used for filming or studying sharks in the wild, and sometimes for purely recreational shark watching. Because of the apparent security afforded by the struc-

Above: Underwater cages afford a level of security from which to observe sharks. However, a determined great white can often terrify the occupants.

ture, they are sometimes used as havens from which to provoke a shark into dramatic action. Some of the most vivid film footage of great white sharks has been recorded in this way.

Nonetheless, many occupants of cages have emerged seriously shaken, both literally and figuratively. Necessarily light and deceptively flimsy structures, they are easily damaged by a determined charge from a massive great white, and attacking great whites are nothing if not determined.

PHOTOGRAPHY

Few wildlife images are quite so potent as that of a large shark on the prowl. Yet photographing sharks, whether with still or movie cameras, is a highly specialized and skilled endeavour.

Perhaps the most disquieting element in shark photography is the need to get close – really close – to your subject. Because of murkiness of even clear ocean waters and the wide angle lenses generally favoured, to fill the frame with even a large shark, the camera must be within 3 or 4 metres (10-13ft) of the subject. Imagine getting that close to a wild tiger!

This need to get close poses the biggest practical problem, because it is surprisingly difficult to approach a free-swimming shark. Most are unexpectedly timid and evasive. Photographers often resort to baiting the water with dead fish or 'chum', which itself can elicit aggressive behaviour. Even if this does not provoke an attack, it can speed up the shark's usual leisurely cruise to the point where high quality photography is again impossible.

Most photographers prefer not to shoot from the sanctuary of a cage, which is intrusive, artificial and particularly subject to turbulence. In recent years 'Neptunic' armour has become popular, allowing photographers the freedom to move in open water with some protection from possible injury. Even so it is scarcely surprising that truly good photographs of large sharks are rare. Professional shark photographers can charge large fees for their best work. Few would deny that they deserve every penny.

QUICK LEARNER

Even laboratory-based shark researchers aren't completely safe from shark attack. In June 1965 at America's Lerner Laboratory, graduate student Karl Kuchnov was preparing to anaesthetise a half-metre (20in) lemon shark, when his subject managed to turn round and sink its teeth into his chest. Fortunately the wound – a neat floret of tiny teeth marks – was not serious.

Below: Divers watch an enormous great white shark from the relative safety of a 'shark-proof' underwater cage.

Above: Photographing a great white.
Below: Valerie Taylor tests a mesh suit
on the jaws of a willing blue shark.

RON & VALERIE TAYLOR

Amongst moving picture photographers, perhaps the best known are the husband and wife team, Ron and Valerie Taylor. This Australian couple have been responsible for filming numerous shark dramas and documentaries, including *Blue Water, White Death* as well as live shark sequences for *Jaws*. They are universally acknowledged as experts in their field, and few people can be as knowledgeable about shark affairs.

Yet even this vast experience cannot afford complete protection. Valerie Taylor has twice been the victim of shark attack. On the last such occasion, a blue shark she was filming inflicted a severe laceration to her leg. The consummate professional, she had the presence of mind to ensure the on-board cameras were rolling before returning to the safety of her boat.

Shark Mythology

MYTHS are, of course, nothing new, although perhaps their nature has changed with the years. From a standpoint close to the 21st Century, it is easy to feel superior to ancient peoples who thought that eclipses signified the end of the world, or that caves were the gateways to hell. But perhaps the awful truth is that the shark is just as terrifying today, whether seen as a fabulous sea monster or merely as the supremely efficient underwater predator we now know it to be.

But whereas European mythology reveals a rich vein of fabulous creatures, from Unicorns to serpent-headed Gorgons, it is only in far-off places that the shark has been so revered. Solomon Islanders, Australian Aborigines and even Pacific Coast American Indians all have tales of shark-gods and the like.

To primitive Hawaiians, the king of the sharks was known as Kamo Hoa Lii, and swam off Honolulu. His queen, Oahu, lived in Pearl Harbour. Like many ancient peoples, the islanders attempted to interact with their gods, either to appease them or to somehow receive part of their power. When the American Naval base was under construction at Pearl Harbour, evidence was found of large shark pens on the sea floor, in which local warriors had once battled with the relatives of Kamo Hoa Lii armed with little more than sticks. The explorer Otto von Kotzebue recorded seeing, in 1820, a large shark kept confined in the mouth of the Pearl River. Humans were sometimes thrown into the shark's pen, although whether as punishment or sacrifice is unclear.

In Japan, where the shark was often a symbol of fear, there was a shark god, the god of storms. In Ceylon during the pearl-diving season, snake-charmers were used to exert a calming influence on the sharks. More unlikely still was the chilling practice of certain Pacific Islanders of shark-kissing. It was believed that once kissed, a shark would be rendered harmless, although the cure sounds infinitely worse than the disease. Would-be kissers were evidently prepared for their underwater seductions on a diet of kava, a naturally-occurring narcotic.

The most widespread and potent shark mythology, however, centres on the archipelagos of the Pacific. To their inhabitants, intrepid sailors in their tiny, fragile canoes, sharks were understandably viewed as creatures of great power – the supernatural kings of the ocean. The natives of New Guinea revere all large sharks as terrible wizards which must not be harmed or caught, whilst Polynesians had a similar taboo about blue sharks.

In Western culture, the shark has rarely been elevated into myth – perhaps because the literal reality is quite horrifying enough. Such legends as do exist were largely confined to the superstitions of mariners who believed, for instance, that sharks could somehow sense the presence of human corpses aboard a ship and would doggedly follow in its wake.

The shark has, however, made fleeting appearances in our fiction, along with *Moby Dick*, the great white whale of Herman Melville and the giant squid of Jules Verne's *20,000 Leagues Under the Sea*.

Most such references have made the common error of over-glamourizing or dramatizing a subject which, to most of us, scarcely needs it. The American writer, Zane Grey (better-known for pulp cowboy novels) wrote several times in sub-Hemingway vein about his exploits big-game fishing. In the thirties, Horace Mazet recounted similar exploits in *Shark! Shark!*, a volume as moderate as the exclamation marks suggest. There have been other, even less measured attempts to cash in on sharks.

From time to time, newspaper accounts highlight shark attacks, either through the absence of more substantial news, or on those rare occasions when attacks are particularly horrific or frequent. Often the urge to sell newspapers overcomes any serious interest in the facts. But the shark event of the century, in the sense that it alerted millions to a species which most of us will never see, was Peter Benchley's 1974 book, *Jaws*, dealt with in detail in the following chapter.

We have sent probes beyond our solar system, yet we know so very little about a creature infinitely closer to home. Even to marine scientists, the shark remains almost as mysterious, and certainly as potent, as ever it was in more primitive times. Perhaps the truth is that, to most of us, the shark prowls on the frontier between consciousness and nightmare, a creature part real, part myth. Perhaps that is the fate of anything so awe-inspiring and so terrible, which can strike so suddenly, inflict such damage and then return without qualm to his dark, mysterious world.

Right: Many cultures have elevated large sharks to the status of gods or wizards. Perhaps it is not surprising that such potent and deadly creatures should be treated with respect normally only afforded to higher beings.

'Jaws'

IN 1974 Peter Benchley's best-selling book, *Jaws* struck an unsuspecting public. The subsequent movie of the same name was an even more spectacular success, breaking all Hollywood box-office records and catapulting director Steven Spielberg into celebrity status. Along the world's shores and beaches the effect was just as profound as the media fell over itself to exploit the film's phenomenal success. Just as *Jaws* depicted a wave of shark hysteria on celluloid, so real bathers on real beaches were starkly reminded of the potential terror below. Few bathers can have ventured into the water without hearing at least an echo of that insistent soundtrack music as *Jaws'* great white shark prepared to attack.

The book, and the subsequent films, raised shark consciousness to unprecedented levels. *Jaws'* great white conformed to the 'rogue shark' theory previously advanced by the Australian shark expert, Victor Coppleson. A single great white is portrayed as making repeated (and increasingly audacious) attacks on bathers and fishermen, including some with the temerity to attempt to catch it. Eventually a team is assembled to track the shark down, only to find that they become the hunted – as their boat is wrecked and their leader eaten alive.

Most shark authorities now believe that such shark behaviour is exceedingly rare, if it occurs at all. Certainly the relentless stalking of human prey depicted in *Jaws'* finale has never been recorded from life. Nonetheless, an otherwise similar series of attacks (see page 28) did take place off New Jersey in 1916, causing hysteria comparable to that in Benchley's imagination.

FACT MORE FRIGHTENING THAN FICTION

In 1974 Peter Benchley, the author of *Jaws* was taking part in the production of a documentary film on sharks off Dangerous Reef on Australia's eastern seaboard. For one sequence, to be filmed by Stan Waterman, one of the team responsible for the celebrated *Blue Water, White Death* four years earlier, Benchley was lowered from a boat in a shark cage. Suddenly a great white estimated to be 4.2 metres (14ft) in length appeared, making particularly violent and insistent attacks on Benchley's flimsy sanctuary. Such was the ferocity of the assault that Waterman feared the cage would not sustain the assault. Fortunately it did, but it was a severely chastened author who returned to the surface.

Above: This still from 'Blue Water, White Death' captures the jaws of a great white.

Above and below: These stills from 'Jaws' movies indicate how mechanical sharks, inter-cut with actual footage of great whites, created cinema sensations that electrified the film-going public.

BRUCE SHARK, SUPERSTAR

'Bruce', the mechanical star of the *Jaws* movie, elevated the great white shark to international stardom. In fact there were three 'Bruces', all created by special effects expert Bob Mattey. Although substantially lighter than a real great white at 1.5 tonnes/tons, to impress the film-going public even more, 'Bruce' was almost one metre (3ft 4in) longer than the largest great white ever reliably recorded. Each cost some $150,000 to make, and thirteen technicians were needed to operate them. 'Bruce' even made it onto the cover of the prestigious American magazine, *Time*.

As well as the mechanical 'Bruce', actual footage of real great whites in action was used in Spielberg's film. Australian under-water film specialists Ron and Valerie Taylor, were commissioned to 'train' great whites to attack near Port Lincoln, South Australia. When the cameras rolled, the sharks responded superbly.

Conclusion

TRUE, man-eating species of shark are perhaps the most voracious and irrepressible carnivores alive on the planet today. But before you cancel all plans to go into the water, consider this: sharks have much more to fear from us than we have of them. An estimated half million tonnes/tons of shark are landed by fishermen each year.

Whatever their status as underwater terrorists and occasional media anti-heroes, sharks are simply one of the more striking elements in the rich variety of the world's fauna. They have as much 'right' to exist as we have. Man finds them useful, both as game and for the products derived from them. They probably have something to teach us if only we understood them better. And who can fail to be moved by their sleek, sensuous grace?

Even as killers, sharks are far, far less lethal to humans than something much closer to our everyday lives – the motor car. Vehicle accidents kill more people every month in the UK alone, than have probably died in all the shark attacks in history. Road accident injuries, too, can be equally terrible. Any traffic policeman can attest that a serious road accident is a scene of such bloody gore as might turn the stomach of even the coldest fish. No doubt road safety could be improved immeasurably if we imagined a hungry great white in the footwell of every car.

So why are the hunters of the deep so much more horrifying in the popular imagination? Cars, whatever their drawbacks, are useful, familiar and comfortable (inside, at least). You can (usually) see them coming and, above all, they are (again, usually) under our control. Sharks, unless you happen to

be a remora (the 'shark sucker' fish that often attach themselves to the under sides of sharks), are anything but. Most of us have never seen a shark in the wild. Most of their victims don't see the one that gets them, either. Their most compelling characteristic, from our point

of view, is their monstrous ability to strike from nowhere and inflict horrible damage . . . like the beast that lurks in the wardrobe of childhood nightmares. Irrational, it may be, but somehow the killer shark strikes a note with our most primitive fears.

Sharks are often mercilessly fished and exploited (above and right) although many serious scientific studies are now being conducted worldwide (left).

SHARK PRODUCTS

FLESH
Although never popular in Europe, in many parts of the world shark meat has been on the menu for centuries. (Dogfish, sometimes sold as rock salmon, is an exception.) It is now becoming more common in trendier restaurants. The flesh is also used as fertilizer.

BLOOD
Shark blood contains anticoagulant compounds valuable in the treatment and prevention of coronary conditions in humans.

LIVER
Like the livers of many fish, those of many species of shark are a rich source of nutrients, notably vitamin A. In humans this is essential for healthy eye development, although synthetic substitutes have reduced demand. Shark liver compounds are also used in cosmetics, paints and certain highly specialised lubricants.

FINS
Sharkfin soup is an exotic oriental dish made from the horny fibres of the dorsal, pectoral and lower caudal fins of many shark species. It will be familiar to visitors to the more exclusive Chinese restaurants.

SKIN
Sharkskin is used in two forms. Shagreen is derived from the skin of certain shark species, mainly rays, in which the dermal denticles are relatively small or absent. Although now largely supplanted by other materials, it was once used for polishing wood or where a non-slip surface was required, such as on the handles of swords.
Shark leather is particularly prized for expensive shoes and other leather products. It is stronger and more flexible than cow hide.

CARTILAGE
Shark cartilage yields a range of biochemicals, including compounds useful in the treatment of burns.

EYE
The corneas of cartilaginous fishes such as the shark are ideally suited for use as human corneal transplants.

JAWS AND TEETH
Shark teeth, in particular, have long been employed for decorative and ceremonial purposes. Eskimos, Maoris and Pacific Islanders have also used shark teeth to make knives and weapons.

The capacity of such a creature as the great white to actually eat us may be terrifying, but it is not unique. Several land-dwelling predators could do that. Nor, at least in some regions, is the ability to strike unseen: we can imagine any number of venomous snakes and insects that might do likewise if we are careless enough to let them, although most people might prefer to be fatally stung than eaten alive.

Perhaps the shark's special terror is its ability to do both: strike without warning, and eat its victim alive. Then there is the sheer violent ferocity of the beast, against which almost no ploy, and certainly no attempt to reason, can work.

Something between 20 and 30 shark attacks on humans are officially recorded each year world-wide, of which the majority are non-fatal. Although some estimates place the true number at nearer 100, since attacks commonly go unreported in remote or under-developed areas, this constitutes an exceptionally low risk. An individual's chances of dying from shark attack in any one year are probably in the region of one in a billion. You are several hundred times more likely to win a sole jackpot in the British national lottery. Perhaps this is one reason why there is no specific word in the English language for shark phobia.

Above: A lemon shark is being tagged by a scientist studying shark behaviour.

Top: A diver feeds a great white shark from an underwater cage.

Right: An inquisitive great white circles an underwater cage.

OTHER KILLERS

There are, however, many other known killers in the world's oceans and seas. Most of us are familiar with jellyfish, and it would be difficult to conceive of an organism less substantial when compared to a charging great white. Yet to be stung by even the relatively harmless specimens common in British waters is an unpleasant experience. The Portuguese Man o' War, occasionally found in English coastal waters, carries a particularly painful sting which has been known to disable swimmers sufficiently to cause drowning. But then, a wasp sting can also kill, if you are one of those rare individuals allergic to it.

The tropical box jellyfish, on the other hand, is a true killer. Its sting causes intense pain and even death.

Even when non-fatal, the venom produces large areas of ugly scarring.

Other less heralded sea-going killers include the scorpion fish, whose gaily-coloured spines carry a potentially fatal sting. The stone fish, hard to spot but easy to tread on, is similarly venomous. Then there is the blue-ringed octopus, a tiny creature no bigger than a matchbox, whose bite can also be fatal.

Nor are rivers and estuaries safe. Every schoolboy has heard of the piranha fish, said to be able to strip a body to the bone in seconds. Although no human fatality has ever been recorded, the red-bellied piranha in particular can be aggressive and inflict a painful bite. This little terror is, on the other hand, easy to catch and reputedly good to eat.

But of all estuary dwellers, crocodiles, alligators and their kin are by far the most intimidating. The huge and very aggressive salt water crocodile (*Crocodylus porosus*), and its slightly smaller cousin, the Nile crocodile, certainly take their toll on human life. This monster, found in northern Australia and south-east Asia, grows to over 8 metres (26ft) in length and exceeds 2 tonnes/tons in weight.

In February 1945 salt water crocodiles are reputed to have taken the lives of approximately 900 Japanese soldiers on Ramree Island, Burma. The toll has since been much disputed, but even half that figure represents perhaps half a century's worth of shark attack fatalities.

But by far the deadliest marine animal is the sea snake, *Astrotia stokesii*. This is not only found in huge numbers in tropical seas, but delivers a poison far more venomous than any land-dwelling snake. The venom of another variety, *Hydrophis belcheri*, has been found to be 100 times more toxic than that of even the most feared land snake, the Australian taipan.

Although sea snakes left to their own devices avoid man, they may be accidentally provoked by fishermen and are widely hunted for their attractive skins. Such is their abundance that they probably harm more humans than all the other sea-borne 'killers' put together. Estimates put the number of fatalities at hundreds per year, especially in the deltas and estuaries of south-east Asia.

But for all these threats from the deep, anyone who ventures down to the sea is wise to bear one other enemy in mind. By far the biggest killer in all the world's oceans is the sea itself.

Left and right: It is worth remembering that shark attacks do not occur often, however, images like these still stimulate one of our most basic instincts – fear.

Index

abalone 51
ampullae of Lorenzini 10, 37
Antoine, Jules 75
Arecki, Mohammed 65
Asai, Iona 74
attacks:
  Africa 58-60
  Australia 47-49
  Europe 61-62
  Great Britain 63
  New Zealand 57
  North America 50-53
  Pacific 54-56
attack, shark 6, 19, 20, 21, 26, 27, 34, 38, 39, 40, 41, 42, 43, 44, 45, 46, 47, 48, 49, 50, 51, 53, 54, 55, 56, 57, 58, 59, 60, 61, 62, 63, 64, 65, 66, 67, 68, 69, 70, 71, 72, 73, 74, 75, 76, 80, 85, 88, 90, 94
Aubone, Alfredo 64
Azores 22

'bang stick' 80
basking shark 11, 14, 63, 68, 82
Benchley, Peter 7, 28, 86, 88
blacktail reef shark 60
blacktip shark 56, 60
blood 19, 27, 30, 31, 34, 44, 60, 64, 67, 72, 73, 91
blue pointer 12, 27
blue shark 11, 12, 19, 21, 32, 37, 39, 49, 53, 56, 57, 60, 76, 85
Blue Water, White Death 85, 88
Bondi Beach 48, 49
bonnet shark 46
Boundy, Ray 21
Bource, Henri 49, 71
Brinkley, Jack 44
bronze whaler 18, 19, 21, 57
bull shark 11, 21, 28, 39, 49, 50, 53, 59, 60

California 27, 50, 51, 53, 57, 58
Calypso 82
cannibalism 14, 33
Cape San Juan 67
Carcharodon carcharias 22, 61
Carcharodon megalodon 8, 9, 29
cartilage 10, 29, 30, 91
Chalor, Manuel 68
Chapel, William 63
chum 34, 84
Churchill, Winston 6
cilia 34
Clarke, Norman 48
Constanzo, Luciano 62
copper shark 19, 49, 60
Copplestone, Sir Victor 57, 88
counter measures 76-81
Cousteau, Jacques 80, 82

dermal denticles 10, 30
Dicks, Troy 69
diver 11, 22, 26, 39, 45, 46, 50, 51, 53, 56, 57, 62, 63, 68, 69, 71, 78, 80, 82, 83, 84
dogfish 11, 91
dolphin 22, 44, 61, 62
Donahue, Frank 69
Dooley, Saburo 55
dorsal fin 9, 12, 14, 30, 39, 91

Dunedin 57
Durban 58, 60
dusky shark 53

Echavarria, Gabriel 64
Edwin T Merridith 67
eggs 16, 32, 33
electrical impulses 10, 37, 38
'electronarcosis' 78
electro-receptors 30, 37
'electrotaxic' 78
emergency packs 73
eyes 37, 91

Fisher, Charles 28
fossils 8, 9, 29, 45, 61
Fox, Rodney 49

Galapagos shark 56
Ganges 40, 67
giant sleepy shark 60
gills 32
Girvan, Norman 44
great white shark 9, 11, 12, 14, 18, 19, 20, 21, 22-29, 31, 32, 33, 37, 39, 40, 41, 42, 43, 45, 46, 48, 49, 50, 51, 53, 54, 56, 57, 59, 60, 61, 62, 64, 69, 70, 73, 83, 85, 89, 90, 92
greenland shark 11, 12
grey nurse shark 7, 21, 32, 60
group attack 44
Gurr, James 58

hammerhead shark 7, 21, 42, 48, 49, 50, 53, 56, 57, 60, 73
Hawkins, Sir John 46
Herodotus 45, 61, 66
Himmrich, Helmut 51
holothurian 77
Horton, Linda 21

Indianapolis, SS 6, 67

Java shark 60
Jaws 7, 22, 26, 27, 28, 34, 45, 50, 85, 86, 88, 89
Johnson, Jimmy 63
Jonah 46
Jones, Len 44
Joslin, Donald 51

Kevlar 80
Kotzebue, Otto von 86

'lamia' 45, 46
lateral line 34
lemon shark 30, 53, 56, 60, 78, 92
Limpopo River 59
Logan, Frank 51

mackerel shark 9, 11, 12, 14, 16, 20, 21, 22, 31, 32
mako 9, 12, 14, 21, 22, 31, 32, 33, 42, 49, 53, 56, 57, 60, 63
man-eaters 10, 12, 18-21, 22, 49, 53, 82, 83, 90
mass attacks 39, 54, 66-67, 72, 73
'mermaid's purse' 32
'meshing' 78
Moby Dick 86
Moitessier, Bernard 55

Mozambique 59
'MS-222' 77
Murphy, Dennis 21

Natal 58, 59, 60
Neptunic 80, 84
nets, shark 48, 60, 76, 77, 78
New Venture 21
Nicaragua, Lake 19
Nova Scotia 66
nurse shark 14, 21, 50, 56, 68, 70, 83

oceanic whitetip shark 15, 50, 60, 53, 56
Oceanographic Research Institute 60
oceanographic research platform 62
olfactory centres 34
oophagy 33
oviparous 14, 16, 32
ovoviviparous 12, 14, 16, 32

Pamperin, Robert 53
pectoral fins 22, 30, 91
pelagic shark 19, 32, 39, 54
Petit Parisien, Le 45, 46
piked dogfish 32
Placoderms 8
Plagiostomi 6
Pliny the Elder 45
porbeagle 22, 42, 53, 63
porpoises 44
provoked attacks 68-70
Pruder, Charles 28
Pruna, Andres 70

Ratubalavu, Sailasa 56
ray 10,
reef shark 11, 41, 53, 56
remora 90
requiem sharks 11, 14
rod-caught records 42
Rodger, Brian 49
rogue shark 21, 28, 88
Rondelet, Guillame 46

Schaper, Hans Joachim 63
seal 22, 50, 51, 54, 55, 62
sea lion 22, 27, 51
senses 34-37
'shark billy' 80
'Shark Chaser' 6, 76, 77
shark-kissing 86
'shark-proof' cage 22, 27, 53, 60, 77, 83, 84, 92
Shark Screen 80
Shark! Shark! 86
Shark Shield 78
sharkskin 30, 68, 73, 76, 80, 82, 91
shark species – main entries
  angelshark 12
  barbeled houndshark 12
  basking shark 15
  blind shark 16
  blue shark 19
  bramble shark 12
  bronze whaler 19
  bullhead shark 16
  bull shark 19
  carpetshark 16
  catshark 14
  copper shark 19
  crocodile shark 15

dogfish 12
false catshark 14
finback catshark 14
frilled shark 12
goblin shark 15
great white shark 22-29
groundshark 12
hammerhead shark 12, 20, 30
houndshark 12
mackerel shark 14
megamouth shark 15
nurse shark 16
raggedtooth shark 15
requiem shark 12
roughshark 12
sand tiger shark 15
sawshark 12
sevengill shark 12
shortfin mako 20
sixgill shark 12
thresher shark 15
tiger shark 19
weasel shark 14
whale shark 16
wobbegong 16
zebra shark 16
Shark Tazer 80
silvertip shark 56, 60
Sithole, Petrus 39
snaggletooth shark 60
spearfishing 27, 44, 49, 54, 55, 56, 57, 64, 68, 69, 70, 73
Speilberg, Steven 45, 88, 89
spotted raggedtooth shark 60
Squalo bianco 62
Stilwell, Lester 28
Strauss, Barbara 60
'super touch' 34
surfboards 27, 54, 58, 59, 62
surfing 18,19, 43, 48, 54, 55, 56, 57, 58
Sydney Harbour 47

Taylor, Ron & Valerie 85, 89
thresher 11, 21, 31, 33, 42, 53, 63
tiburon 6, 46
tiger shark 8, 11, 12, 20, 21, 41, 42, 44, 49, 57, 50, 53, 54, 56, 59, 60, 74, 75, 77, 83
tooth bed 33
Troy, Joseph 50
turtle 22, 54
20,000 Leagues Under the Sea 86

Valerian 66
VanZant, Charles 28
victims 71-75
viviparous 12

Weaver, Billy 56
whale shark 11, 68, 82
'white death' 12, 15-29
white pointer 27
Wilson, Barry 53
wind surfer 62
wobbegong 21
World War II 6

xoc 46

Zambezi shark 19, 39, 49, 59